Edited by J. Max Patrick
UNIVERSITY OF FLORIDA

Selected Essays

OF

Francis Bacon

Appleton–Century–Crofts, Inc.
NEW YORK

MANUFACTURED IN THE UNITED STATES OF AMERICA

574-3

Contents

Introduction

Francis Bacon was born in 1561, the third year of Queen Elizabeth's reign. His father, Nicholas, was Lord Keeper, the chief law officer of England. His mother, Anne, was distinguished by rigid Calvinism, a love for household affairs and gardens, and great learning. Her brother-in-law was William Cecil, later Lord Burghley, who became Elizabeth's chief minister. Undaunted by this array of talents, young Francis emulated father, mother, and uncle alike, and "took all knowledge to be his province." After private tutoring at home, he entered Trinity College, Cambridge, at the then customary age—twelve. The subjects taught were traditional ones: theology, law, the philosophy of Plato and Aristotle, medicine based on Galen and Hippocrates, dialectic (the art of logical disputation and discrimination of truth from error), rhetoric, Greek, Hebrew, and mathematics (which included arithmetic, geometry, cosmography, and astronomy). However, Bacon found the dominant Aristotelian philosophy unfruitful and withdrew after less than three years.

In 1576 he was admitted to Gray's Inn, a law school, but departed in 1577 to accompany the English ambassador to France. In Paris, besides gaining experience in diplomacy, he probably became interested in the experimental scientific method advocated and practiced by Bernard Palissy, for from about this time Bacon was an exponent of experiment in science. The sudden death of his father in 1579 recalled him to his legal studies and left him with little income. It was not until 1586 that he was enrolled as a Bencher or barrister entitled to practice law, but from 1584 to 1613 he was a member of Parliament. Unfortunately for his career, he antagonized the queen by opposing her desire for increased taxes. Nevertheless, he won the patronage of her favorite, Robert, Earl of Essex, who made use of Bacon's abilities and good sense, and in return not only attempted to advance him to various offices but endowed him with land worth £1800 (about $60,000 today). Essex attempted to pacify rebellious Ireland, on Bacon's advice, and failed. Disgraced and disgruntled, the earl then rashly plotted a revolt against the English government. When he was charged with treason, Bacon did not refuse to participate in prosecuting him. As a result, Bacon has been condemned for deserting Essex. However, he may deserve praise for putting loyalty to his country above a friendship of convenience. Certainly few Americans would refuse to inform against a friend who became a fifth columnist. In any case, Bacon's career might have been endangered had he acted otherwise, and his mainspring was a desire to gain high office so that he could effect grand schemes to advance knowledge, human welfare, and his own fame.

After James I came to the throne in 1603, Bacon promoted a compromise in Parliament between advocates and opponents of certain disputed royal powers. As a result, the king appointed him Learned Counsel and gave him an annual pension, whereupon Bacon dedicated the *Advancement of Learning* to him.

In the next year, when Bacon was forty-five, he married the well-dowered Alice Barnham, "an alderman's daughter, a handsome maiden, much to my liking." His "rising unto place" continued as he became successively Solicitor General, Attorney General, Lord Keeper, and Lord Chancellor, an eminence equivalent to headship of the United States Supreme Court. He was created Baron Verulam of Verulam in 1618, and Viscount St. Albans in 1621, the year which saw publication of his great work *Novum Organum* (The New Method). This was the second part of his *Instauratio Magna* (The Great Restoration of the Sciences), a project never completed.

Bacon was at the pinnacle of success, but he found the standing slippery. The political faction with which he was associated fell from office, whereupon the new faction determined to oust him from his powerful judicial position. It was not difficult to prove that Bacon, like other judges of the period, had received presents from persons whose legal suits were to be tried by him. Accordingly, he was found guilty of accepting bribes, nominally fined, imprisoned briefly, and disqualified for public office. In his retirement he turned to literature, philosophy, and science and rediscovered the joys of gardening. He published a *History of Henry VII; A History of Life and Death;* a Latin redaction of the *Advancement of Learning; Apothegms; Translations of Certain Psalms;* the third edition of his *Essays;* and (posthumously) *Sylva Sylva-*

rum (A Wood of Woods), and *New Atlantis*. He died on April 9, 1626.

Bacon is now regarded as a father of experimental science, a master of statecraft, a genius in philosophy, an outstanding legalist, and a great essayist. However, Pope condemned him as "the wisest, brightest, meanest of mankind," for it is easy to point to inconsistencies between his selfish, rather ruthless climb to great place and his professions of high ideals. Such dualism was common in his period. Although he may be condemned for sycophancy, possible perversion of justice, ingratitude, extravagance, and carelessness, it must be remembered that he was no sycophant when he gained Elizabeth's enmity by opposing increased taxation; that his record as a judge compares favorably with others of his time; that he not infrequently resisted pressure brought upon him to pervert justice; and that his extravagance in money was offset by his economy in time: as his chaplain recorded, "he suffered no moment nor fragment of time to pass away unprofitably."

Bacon's first collection of essays appeared in 1597. Of its three divisions, the first was devoted to ten "fragments," as he called them: brief discussions of worldly prudence as it concerned a scholar and gentleman. The second part, *Meditationes Sacrae* (Sacred Meditations) treated such themes as atheism and heresy. The third, *Colors of Good and Evil*, analysed popular sayings and gave arguments for and against them. Thus the volume had a unity of tone. Characteristically, the chief topic was prudence, the art of getting on in the world. Equally typical were his tendency to give arguments on both sides of a question and his stress on the useful and expedient.

The volume caused no great stir, for discussions on morals and politics were already common. Humanists had long gathered maxims about statescraft and public life, grouping them under headings in commonplace books. From such groupings, essays easily emerged. For example, "small discourses on dissembling, vanity," and the like had appeared in the anonymous *Remedies against Discontentment* (1596). Thus Bacon was developing an already growing literary genre. However, the form had yet to mature: his early essays are like crude paragraphs of finely-phrased notebook-jottings: they are aphoristic, terse, and elliptical, but deficient in artistic continuity and elaboration.

The "fragments" in the first edition correspond to the essays later numbered 28, 30, 32, 47 through 52, and 55. Twenty-four additional essays were included in a manuscript prepared between 1607 and 1612 but never published. In a letter prefaced to it, Bacon states that he chose to write not long treatises but "certain brief notes, set down rather significantly than curiously [elaborately], which I have called *Essays.*" He borrowed the term, which means *an attempt, trial,* or *assay,* from Montaigne. Bacon adds that the word is recent, but the thing, ancient, "for Seneca's *Epistles to Lucilius,* if you mark them well, are but essays, that is, dispersed meditations." Despite such classical precedents, Bacon's perfecting of the essay form was largely due to its popularization by minor writers like William Cornwallis and by the wide circulation of Bacon's own original "fragments."

In the second edition, essays 25 and 55 were omitted, but the following were added: 2, 7, 8, 11, 13, 14, 16, 17, 19, 20, 23, 25, 26, 27, 34, 36, 38, 39, 40, 42, 43, 44, and 53. The nature of the contents was made more explicit by a new title, *Essays or Counsels Civil and Moral,* and by a dedicatory epistle in which Bacon points out that the essays "come home to men's business and bosoms," adding that he enlarged them "both in number and weight so that they are indeed a new work." A Latin translation, published posthumously as *Sermones Fideles, sive Interiorem Rerum* (Trustworthy Adages, or the Secrets of Things), throws light on the meaning of many doubtful passages. Bacon thought that this version would "last as long as books last," because it was written in the universal language.

The style of the latest essays is smoother, less contracted, and more coherent than that of the original ones. Transitions are eased, and more illustrative material is inserted. Furthermore, the early essays are expanded and revised, with gains in clarity and forcefulness. In them, the essay form had been brought to maturity, and Bacon had made the greatest contribution to its development.

The subject of Bacon's essays was reality, not life as it might be or ought to be, but as it is. He was writing a handbook for success in a world of mixed good and evil, a guide which might well be entitled *How to Make the Most of Men and Opportunities in a Competitive Society*. In politics he was conservative, opportunistic, and rather unsystematic. He advocated rule by an intelligent king limited by nobles whose powers were not dangerously great. Government he regarded as the difficult art whereby rulers give people what is good for them. He identified the interests of a king and the welfare of a nation and its people, though he condemned democracy and failed to see the potentialities of the House of Commons. His ideal government was one which kept the people happy and prosperous, promoted science, regulated excess and waste, protected infant industries, maintained military strength, and prevented a concentration of wealth in the hands of a few. He advocated a strong foreign policy, believed that war vitalized a state, urged the union of Scotland and England, and recommended the formation of colonies. In religious matters he was cautious, Erastian, and outwardly devout. In worldly matters, his standard of judgment was utilitarian.

To the objection that Bacon failed to practice what he preached, the answer may be given that he was intelligent enough to see his errors and to warn against them, as when he wrote upon bribery. Likewise, if it is objected that his ideas are often trite and obvious, there is a ready reply: the obvious is likely to be overlooked; a great merit of the essays is that they state the commonplace memorably and strikingly, forcing men to reconsider their darling opinions.

The present selection of significant essays is based on the 1625 text collated with the best subsequent editions. Spelling and punctuation have been modernized as far as the sense permits. All dates are A.D. unless otherwise specified. In footnotes, d. means *died,* and n. means *note*. Other abbreviations are standard ones.

Principal Dates in Francis Bacon's Life

1561 Francis Bacon was born in London on January 22.
1573 Matriculated at Trinity College, Cambridge.
1576 Admitted into Gray's Inn.
1577-1579 In France with the English Ambassador.
1582 Admitted to the bar.
1584 Entered Parliament as Member for Melcombe.
1587 *Execution of Mary Queen of Scots.*
1588 *Destruction of the Spanish Armada.*
1597 First edition of the *Essays.*
1601 *Execution of the Earl of Essex.*
1603 *Death of Queen Elizabeth and accession of James I.* Bacon knighted.
1605 Publication of *The Advancement of Learning.*
1606 Bacon married Alice Barnham.
1607 Solicitor General. *Colonization of Virginia.*
1610 Death of his mother. *Thermometer invented.*
1611 *Publication of the Authorized Version of the Bible.*
1612 Second edition of the *Essays.*
1613 Attorney General.
1614 *Napier invents logarithms.*
1616 Privy Counsellor.
1617 Lord Keeper.
1618 Lord High Chancellor and Baron Verulam of Verulam.
1620 Publication of *Novum Organum.*
1621 Viscount St. Albans. Retirement to Gorhambury in disgrace.
1622 Publication of *Henry VII.*
1625 Third edition of the *Essays.*
1626 Died on April 9. Publication of *New Atlantis.*
1638 Latin edition of the *Essays.*

THE ESSAYS

I. OF TRUTH

"What is truth?" said jesting Pilate,[1] and would not stay for an answer. Certainly there be that delight in giddiness[2] and count it a bondage to fix a belief; affecting[3] free-will in thinking as well as in acting. And though the sects of philosophers of that kind[4] be gone, yet there remain certain discoursing wits[5] which are of the same veins, though there be not so much blood in them as was in those of the ancients. But it is not only the difficulty and labor which men take in finding out of truth, nor again that when it is found it imposeth upon men's thoughts, that doth bring lies in favor, but a natural though corrupt love of the lie itself. One of the later school of the Grecians[6] examineth the matter and is at a stand to think what should be in it, that men should love lies where neither they make for pleasure, as with poets,[7] nor for advantage, as with the merchant, but for the lies' sake. But I cannot tell. This same truth is a naked and open daylight that doth not show the masks and mummeries and triumphs of the world half so stately and daintily[8] as candlelights. Truth may perhaps come to the price of a pearl, that showeth best by day; but it will not rise to the price of a diamond or carbuncle, that showeth best in varied lights. A mixture of a lie doth ever add pleasure. Doth any man doubt that if there were taken out of men's minds vain opinions, flattering hopes, false valuations, imaginations as one would, and the like, but it would leave the minds of a number of men poor shrunken things, full of melancholy and indisposition, and unpleasing to themselves? One of the fathers,[9] in great severity, called poesy *vinum daemonum* [the wine of devils] because it filleth the

1. Roman administrator in Judea who delivered Jesus to be crucified. In the Latin text of the *Essays,* Pilate is called *derisor,* a mocking or cynical person; he stands for cynical skepticism as opposed to Jesus, who stands for truth. 2. Whirling from idea to idea. 3. Aiming at. 4. Skeptics like Pyrrho, d. 275 B.C., who taught that men cannot know truth. 5. Talkative, rambling minds. 6. Lucian, Greek satirist, d. 200. 7. B. uses *lies* in the broadest sense, including fictitious writing. 8. Elegantly. Cf. XXXVII. 9. Probably St. Augustine, who calls poetry "the wine of error."

imagination and yet it is but the shadow of a lie. But it is not
30 the lie that passeth through the mind, but the lie that sinketh in and settleth in it that doth the hurt, such as we spake of before. But howsoever these things are thus in men's depraved judgments and affections, yet truth, which only doth judge itself, teacheth that the inquiry of truth, which is the love-making or wooing of it; the knowledge of truth, which is the presence of it; and the belief of truth, which is the enjoying of it, is the sovereign good of human nature. The first creature [10] of God in the works of the days was the light of the sense; the last was the light of reason: and his sabbath work ever since is the
40 illumination of his Spirit. First he breathed light upon the face of the matter or chaos; then he breathed light into the face of man; and still he breatheth and inspireth light into the face of his chosen. The poet that beautified the sect that was otherwise inferior to the rest,[11] saith yet excellently well: "It is a pleasure to stand upon the shore and to see ships tossed upon the sea; a pleasure to stand in the window of a castle and to see a battle and the adventures thereof below: but no pleasure is comparable to the standing upon the vantage ground of truth," (a hill not to be commanded,[12] and where the air is always clear
50 and serene), "and to see the errors and wanderings and mists and tempests in the vale below"; so [13] always that this prospect be with pity and not with swelling or pride. Certainly it is heaven upon earth to have a man's mind move in charity, rest in providence, and turn upon the poles of truth.[14]

To pass from theological and philosophical truth to the truth of civil business: [15] it will be acknowledged, even by those that practice it not, that clear and round [16] dealing is the honor of man's nature and that mixture of falsehood is like alloy in coin

10. Created thing. See *Genesis,* i, 3 and 7. 11. Lucretius the Roman poet, was the ornament of the Epicurean group of philosophers: they taught that pleasure is the aim of life. 12. Not to be looked down upon by others. 13. Provided. 14. When a man's mind looks to charity as the motivation of his actions, when he confines his deeds within the limits set by universal Providence, and when he lives and acts with constant reference to truth. B. writes in terms of Ptolemaic astronomy which taught that there were ten heavens or spheres of space enclosing the earth. The tenth sphere, known as the *Primum Mobile* or First Movable, gave motion to the other spheres. Thus it "moved" the universe. At the same time it enclosed the universe from absolute space, in which it "rested" or was motionless. All the spheres rotated about fixed poles. 15. From truth in the abstract to truthfulness in practical affairs. 16. Honest.

of gold and silver, which may make the metal work the better, but it embaseth it. For these winding and crooked courses are the goings of the serpent, which goeth basely upon the belly and not upon the feet. There is no vice that doth so cover a man with shame as to be found false and perfidious. And therefore Montaigne[17] saith prettily when he enquired the reason why the word of the lie should be in such disgrace and such an odious charge. Saith he, "If it be well weighed, to say that a man lieth is as much to say as that he is brave towards God and a coward towards men." For a lie faces God and shrinks from man. Surely the wickedness of falsehood and breach of faith cannot possibly be so highly expressed as in that it shall be the last peal to call the judgments of God upon the generations of men, it being foretold that when Christ cometh, "He shall not find faith upon the earth."[18]

II. OF DEATH

Men fear death as children fear to go in the dark; and, as that natural fear in children is increased with tales, so is the other. Certainly the contemplation of death as the wages of sin and passage to another world is holy and religious, but the fear of it, as a tribute due unto nature, is weak. Yet in religious meditations there is sometimes mixture of vanity and superstition. You shall read in some of the friars' books of mortification[1] that a man should think with himself what the pain is if he have but his finger's end pressed or tortured, and thereby imagine what the pains of death are when the whole body is corrupted and dissolved; when many times death passeth with less pain than the torture of a limb; for the most vital parts are not the quickest of sense. And by him that spake only as a philosopher and natural man,[2] it was well said: *Pompa mortis magis terret quam mors ipsa.* [The trappings of death terrify us more than death itself.] Groans and convulsions and a discolored face, and friends weeping, and blacks and ob-

17. French essayist, d. 1592, from whose *Essais* B. derived the word "essay." 18. *Luke* xviii, 8. 1. Books about repressing fleshly desires. 2. Seneca, philosopher and dramatist, d. 65, speaking in ignorance of the supernatural revelations of Christianity.

sequies and the like show death terrible. It is worthy the observing that there is no passion in the mind of man so weak
20 but it mates[3] and masters the fear of death; and therefore death is no such terrible enemy, when a man hath so many attendants about him that can win the combat of him:[4] revenge triumphs over death; love slights it; honor aspireth to it; grief flieth to it; fear preoccupateth it. Nay, we read,[5] after Otho the emperor had slain himself, pity (which is the tenderest of affections) provoked many to die out of mere compassion to their sovereign, and as the truest sort of followers. Nay, Seneca[6] adds niceness[7] and satiety: *Cogita quamdiu eadem feceris; mori velle, non tantum fortis, aut miser, sed*
30 *etiam fastidiosus potest.* [Consider how long you have been doing the same things: the desire to die may be felt not only by the brave or the miserable but also by the fastidious.] A man would die, though he were neither valiant nor miserable, only upon weariness to do the same thing so oft over and over. It is no less worthy to observe how little alteration in good spirits the approaches of death make, for they appear to be the same men till the last instant. Augustus Caesar[8] died in a compliment: *Livia, conjugii nostri memor, vive et vale* [Livia, mindful of our marriage, live on, and fare thee well];
40 Tiberius[9] in dissimulation, as Tacitus[10] saith of him: *Iam Tiberium vires et corpus, non dissimulatio, deserebant* [For bodily strength and vitality were now deserting Tiberius, but not his duplicity]; Vespasian[11] in a jest, sitting upon the stool: *Ut puto Deus fio* [I suppose I am becoming a God]; Galba[12] with a sentence: *Feri, si ex re sit populi Romani* [Strike, if it be for the good of the Roman people], holding forth his neck; Septimius Severus[13] in dispatch: *Adeste si quid mihi restat agendum* [Be ready if anything remains to be done by me]; and the like. Certainly the Stoics[14] bestowed
50 too much food upon death and by their great preparations made it appear more fearful. Better saith he[15] *qui finem vitae extremum inter munera ponat naturae* [who regards the conclusion of life as one of nature's blessings]. It is as nat-

3. Overpowers. 4. From him (Death). 5. We read in Plutarch's *Lives* that. 6. See n. 2. 7. Fastidiousness. 8. First Roman emperor, d. 14. 9. Second Roman emperor, d. 37. 10. Roman historian. 11. Roman emperor, d. 79. 12. Roman emperor, d. 69, killed by his soldiers. 13. Roman emperor, d. 211. 14. Followers of Zeno, d. 264, who advocated indifference to riches, pain, health, passion and even life itself. 15. Juvenal, d. 125?, satiric poet.

ural to die as to be born; and to a little infant, perhaps, the one is as painful as the other. He that dies in earnest pursuit is like one that is wounded in hot blood, who for a time scarce feels the hurt; and therefore a mind fixed and bent upon somewhat that is good doth avert the dolors of death. But above all, believe it, the sweetest canticle is *Nunc dimittis* [Now lettest thou (thy servant) depart (in peace)],[16] when a man hath 60 obtained worthy ends and expectations. Death hath this also, it openeth the gate to good fame, and extinguisheth envy. *Extinctus amabitur idem* [That very man will be loved—when he is dead].

IV. OF REVENGE

Revenge is a kind of wild justice, which the more man's nature runs to, the more ought law to weed it out. For as for the first wrong, it doth but offend the law; but the revenge of that wrong putteth the law out of office. Certainly in taking revenge a man is but even with his enemy, but in passing it over he is superior, for it is a prince's part to pardon. And Solomon, I am sure, saith: "It is the glory of a man to pass by an offence."[1] That which is past is gone and irrevocable, and wise men have enough to do with things present and to come: therefore they do but trifle with themselves that labor in past 10 matters. There is no man doth a wrong for the wrong's sake but thereby to purchase himself profit or pleasure or honor or the like. Therefore why should I be angry with a man for loving himself better than me? And if any man should do wrong merely out of ill-nature, why yet it is but like the thorn or briar which prick and scratch because they can do no other. The most tolerable sort of revenge is for those wrongs which there is no law to remedy: but then let a man take heed the revenge be such as there is no law to punish; else a man's enemy is still beforehand, and it is two for one.[2] Some, when 20 they take revenge, are desirous the party should know whence it cometh. This is the more generous, for the delight seemeth

16. *Luke* ii, 29. 1. *Proverbs* xix, 11. 2. Otherwise the enemy receives only one injury, but the avenger bears two: the original injury and legal punishment for his act of vengeance.

to be not so much in doing the hurt as in making the party repent. But base and crafty cowards are like the arrow that flieth in the dark. Cosmus, Duke of Florence,[3] had a desperate saying against perfidious or neglecting friends, as if those wrongs were unpardonable: "You shall read," saith he, "that we are commanded to forgive our enemies; but you never read that we are commanded to forgive our friends." But yet the
30 spirit of Job was in better tune: "Shall we," saith he, "take good at God's hands and not be content to take evil also?" And so of friends in a proportion. This is certain: that a man that studieth revenge keeps his own wounds green, which otherwise would heal and do well. Public revenges are for the most part fortunate, as that for the death of Caesar, for the death of Pertinax, for the death of Henry the Third of France,[4] and many more; but in private revenges it is not so. Nay rather, vindictive persons live the life of witches, who, as they are mischievous, so end they infortunate.

V. OF ADVERSITY

It was a high speech of Seneca (after the manner of the Stoics), "that the good things which belong to prosperity are to be wished, but the good things that belong to adversity are to be admired":[1] *Bona rerum secundarum optabilia; adversarum mirabilia.* Certainly if miracles be the command over nature, they appear most in adversity.[2] It is yet a higher speech of his than the other (much too high for a heathen): "It is true greatness to have in one the frailty of a man and the security of a God." *Vere magnum habere fragilitatem hominis,*
10 *securitatem hominis, securitatem Dei.* This would have done better in poesy, where transcendencies are more allowed. And the poets indeed have been busy with it, for it is in effect the

3. Cosmo de' Medici, d. 1574. 4. Julius Caesar's murder was avenged by Mark Antony and Augustus, with the result that Augustus ultimately became Emperor. The mutineers who murdered the emperor Pertinax in 193 were put to death by Septimius Severus, the next emperor. Henry III was assassinated in 1589 by a monk, who was killed forthwith. 1. Wondered at. See II, n. 2, n. 14. 2. If miracles mean command over nature, then they appear most in times of adversity when men control their natures.

thing which is figured in that strange fiction of the ancient poets, which seemeth not to be without mystery;[3] nay, and to have some approach to the state of a Christian: that "Hercules, when he went to unbind Prometheus" (by whom human nature is represented), "sailed the length of the great ocean in an earthen pot or pitcher"; lively describing Christian resolution, that saileth in the frail bark of the flesh through the waves of the world. But to speak in a mean:[4] the virtue of prosperity is temperance; the virtue of adversity is fortitude, which, in morals, is the more heroical virtue. Prosperity is the blessing of the Old Testament; adversity is the blessing of the New; which carrieth the greater benediction and the clearer revelation of God's favor. Yet even in the Old Testament, if you listen to David's harp you shall hear as many hearse-like airs as carols; and the pencil of the Holy Ghost hath labored more in describing the afflictions of Job than the felicities of Solomon. Prosperity is not without many fears and distastes, and adversity is not without comforts and hopes. We see in needleworks and embroideries it is more pleasing to have a lively work upon a sad and solemn ground than to have a dark and melancholy work upon a lightsome ground: judge therefore of the pleasure of the heart by the pleasure of the eye. Certainly virtue is like precious odors, most fragrant when they are incensed or crushed; for prosperity doth best discover vice, but adversity doth best discover virtue.

VI. OF SIMULATION AND DISSIMULATION

Dissimulation is but a faint kind of policy or wisdom, for it asketh a strong wit[1] and a strong heart to know when to tell truth, and to do it. Therefore it is the weaker sort of politics[2] that are the great dissemblers.

3. Prometheus, having stolen fire from heaven for mankind, was chained to a rock, where an eagle daily consumed his liver until Hercules killed the bird and released him. The "mystery" or hidden meaning is explained in B.'s *Wisdom of the Ancients,* XXVI: "The voyage of Hercules especially, sailing in a pitcher to set Prometheus free, seems to represent an image of God the Word [Christ] hastening in the frail vessel of the flesh to redeem the human race." 4. In a moderate way. 1. Understanding. 2. Politicians.

Tacitus[3] saith, "Livia sorted[4] well with the arts of her husband and dissimulation of her son," attributing arts or policy to Augustus, and dissimulation to Tiberius. And again, when Mucianus encourageth Vespasian[5] to take arms against Vitellius, he saith, "We rise not against the piercing judgment of Augustus, nor the extreme caution or closeness of Tiberius." These properties of arts or policy, and dissimulation or closeness are indeed habits and faculties several,[6] and to be distinguished. For if a man have that penetration of judgment as[7] he can discern what things are to be laid open, and what to be secreted, and what to be showed at half lights, and to whom and when (which indeed are arts of state and arts of life, as Tacitus well calleth them), to him a habit of dissimulation is a hinderance and a poorness. But if a man cannot obtain to that judgment, then it is left to him generally to be close, and a dissembler. For where a man cannot choose or vary in particulars,[8] there it is good to take the safest and wariest way in general, like the going softly by one that cannot well see. Certainly the ablest men that ever were have had all an openness and frankness of dealing, and a name of certainty and veracity; but then they were like horses well managed, for they could tell passing well when to stop or turn; and at such times when they thought the case indeed required dissimulation, if then they used it, it came to pass that the former opinion spread abroad of their good faith and clearness of dealing made them almost invisible.

There be three degrees of this hiding and veiling of a man's self. The first: closeness, reservation, and secrecy, when a man leaveth himself without observation or without hold to be taken what he is. The second: dissimulation, in the negative, when a man lets fall signs and arguments that he is not that he is. And the third: simulation, in the affirmative, when a man industriously[9] and expressly feigns and pretends to be that he is not.

For the first of these, secrecy, it is indeed the virtue of a confessor. And assuredly the secret man heareth many confessions. For who will open himself to a blab or a babbler? But if a man be thought secret, it inviteth discovery,[10] as the more

3. Roman historian: *Annals,* V. 1. 4. Accorded. Livia was wife of Augustus and mother of Tiberius, the first Roman emperors. 5. Roman emperor. 6. Distinct. 7. Of such a nature that. 8. To suit particular instances. 9. Purposely. 10. Disclosures.

close air sucketh in the more open. And as in confession the revealing is not for worldly use but for the ease of a man's heart, so secret men come to the knowledge of many things in that kind,[11] while men rather discharge their minds than impart their minds. In few words, mysteries are due to secrecy. Besides (to say truth) nakedness is uncomely, as well in mind as body; and it addeth no small reverence to men's manners and actions, if they be not altogether open. As for talkers and futile[12] persons, they are commonly vain[13] and credulous withal; for he that talketh what he knoweth will also talk what he knoweth not. Therefore set it down, "that an habit of secrecy is both politic and moral." And in this part it is good that a man's face give his tongue leave to speak. For the discovery of a man's self by the tracts[14] of his countenance is a great weakness and betraying, by how much it is many times more marked and believed than a man's words.

For the second, which is dissimulation, it followeth many times upon secrecy by a necessity; so that he that will be secret must be a dissembler in some degree. For men are too cunning to suffer a man to keep an indifferent carriage between both, and to be secret, without swaying the balance on either side. They will so beset a man with questions, and draw him on, and pick it out of him, that, without an absurd silence, he must show an inclination one way; or if he do not, they will gather as much by his silence as by his speech. As for equivocations or oraculous[15] speeches, they cannot hold out long. So that no man can be secret, except[16] he give himself a little scope of dissimulation, which is, as it were, but the skirts or train of secrecy.

But for the third degree, which is simulation and false profession, that I hold more culpable, and less politic, except it be in great and rare matters. And therefore a general custom of simulation (which is this last degree) is a vice, rising either of a natural falseness or fearfulness, or of a mind that hath some main faults, which because a man must needs disguise, it maketh him practise simulation in other things, lest his hand should be out of ure.[17]

The great advantages of simulation and dissimulation are three. First, to lay asleep opposition and to surprise. For where

11. In the same way (through confessions). 12. Leaky; i.e., persons who cannot keep a secret. 13. Light-minded. 14. Traits; features. 15. Ambiguous. 16. Unless. 17. Use.

a man's intentions are published, it is an alarum to call up all that are against them. The second is, to reserve to a man's self a fair retreat. For if a man engage himself by a manifest declaration, he must go through or take a fall. The third is, the better to discover the mind of another. For to him that opens himself men will hardly show themselves adverse, but will (fair)[18] let him go on, and turn their freedom of speech to freedom of thought. And therefore it is a good shrewd proverb of the Spaniard, "Tell a lie and find a truth"; as if there were no way of discovery but by simulation. There be also three disadvantages, to set it even. The first, that simulation and dissimulation commonly carry with them a show of fearfulness, which in any business doth spoil the feathers of round flying up to the mark.[19] The second, that it puzzleth and perplexeth the conceits [20] of many that perhaps would otherwise co-operate with him, and makes a man walk almost alone to his own ends. The third and greatest is, that it depriveth a man of one of the most principal instruments for action, which is trust and belief. The best composition and temperature [21] is to have openness in fame and opinion,[22] secrecy in habit, dissimulation in seasonable use, and a power to feign, if there be no remedy.

VII. OF PARENTS AND CHILDREN

The joys of parents are secret, and so are their griefs and fears. They cannot utter the one, nor they will not utter the other.[1] Children sweeten labors, but they make misfortunes more bitter. They increase the cares of life, but they mitigate the remembrance of death. The perpetuity by generation is common to beasts, but memory, merit and noble works are proper to men. And surely a man shall see the noblest works and foundations have proceeded from childless men, which have sought to express the images of their minds where those of their bodies have failed. So the care of posterity is most in

18. Just. 19. Ruffle the feathers of an arrow so that it will no longer fly directly to the target. 20. Thoughts. 21. Temperament. 22. A reputation for frankness. 1. The Latin reads: "Certainly they lack words adequate to express the one, and they are unwilling to publish the other."

them that have no posterity. They that are the first raisers of their houses are most indulgent towards their children, beholding them as the continuance not only of their kind but of their work: and so, both children and creatures.

The difference in affection of parents towards the several children is many times unequal and sometimes unworthy, especially in the mother. As Solomon saith, "A wise son rejoiceth the father, but an ungracious son shames the mother." A man shall see, where there is a house full of children, one or two of the eldest respected,[2] and the youngest made wantons;[3] 20 but in the midst some that are as it were forgotten, who many times nevertheless prove the best. The illiberality of parents in allowance towards their children is a harmful error, makes them base, acquaints them with shifts, makes them sort[4] with mean company, and makes them surfeit the more when they come to plenty. And therefore the proof is best when men keep their authority towards their children but not their purse. Men have a foolish manner (both parents and school masters and servants) in creating and breeding an emulation between brothers during childhood, which many times sorteth to[5] discord when they are men, and disturbeth families. The Italians 30 make little difference between children and nephews or near kinsfolks; but so they be of the lump, they care not though they pass not through their own body. And, to say truth, in nature it is much a like matter, insomuch that we see a nephew sometimes resembleth an uncle or a kinsman more than his own parent, as the blood happens. Let parents choose betimes the vocations and courses they mean their children should take, for then they are most flexible; and let them not too much apply themselves to the disposition of their children 40 as thinking they will take best to that which they have most mind to. It is true that if the affection[6] or aptness of the children be extraordinary, then it is good not to cross it. But generally the precept is good: *optimum elige suave et facile illud faciet consuetudo* [choose what is best, for habit will make it pleasant and easy]. Younger brothers are commonly fortunate,[7] but seldom or never where the elder are disinherited.

2. Favored. 3. Spoiled. 4. Associate. 5. Results in. 6. Inclination.
7. Successful. Estates were usually left to the eldest son.

VIII. OF MARRIAGE AND SINGLE LIFE

He that hath wife and children hath given hostages to fortune,[1] for they are impediments to great enterprises either of virtue or mischief. Certainly the best works and of greatest merit for the public have proceeded from the unmarried or childless men,[2] which both in affection and means have married and endowed the public. Yet it were great reason that those that have children should have greatest care of future times, unto which they must transmit their dearest pledges. Some there are who, though they lead a single life, yet their thoughts do end with themselves, and account future times impertinences.[3] Nay, there are some other that [4] account wife and children but as bills of charges. Nay more, there are some foolish rich covetous men that take a pride in having no children because they may be thought so much the richer. For perhaps they have heard some talk, "Such an one is a great rich man"; and another except to it, "Yea, but he hath a great charge of children," as if it were an abatement to his riches. But the most ordinary cause of a single life is liberty, especially in certain self-pleasing and humorous [5] minds which are so sensible of every restraint as [6] they will go near to think their girdles and garters to be bonds and shackles. Unmarried men are best friends, best masters, best servants; but not always best subjects, for they are light to run away; and almost all fugitives are of this condition. A single life doth well with churchmen, for charity will hardly water the ground where it must first fill a pool.[7] It is indifferent for judges and magistrates; for if they be facile [8] and corrupt, you shall have a servant five times worse than a wife. For soldiers, I find the generals commonly in their hortatives put men in mind of their wives and children; and I think the despising of marriage amongst the Turks maketh the vulgar soldier more base. Certainly wife and children are a kind of discipline of humanity; and single men, though they may be many times

1. They are like hostages who prosper or suffer according to his good or bad fortunes. 2. B. married late and had no children. 3. Matters which do not concern them. 4. Some others who. 5. Eccentric. 6. That. 7. Clergymen will lack means to help their parishioners (the ground) if they must first devote their wealth to filling the needs of their families (the pool). 8. Easy to bribe.

more charitable because their means are less exhaust,[9] yet, on the other side, they are more cruel and hardhearted (good to make severe inquisitors) because their tenderness is not so oft called upon. Grave natures, led by custom and therefore constant, are commonly loving husbands, as was said of Ulysses: *vetulam suam praetulit immortaliti* [he preferred his old wife to immortality].[10] Chaste women are often proud and froward, as presuming upon the merit of their chastity. It is one of the best bonds both of chastity and obedience in the wife if she think her husband wise, which she will never do if she find him jealous. Wives are young men's mistresses, companions for middle age, and old men's nurses. So as a man may have a quarrel to marry when he will.[11] But yet he was reputed one of the wise men that made answer to the question, when a man should marry: "A young man not yet; an elder man not at all."[12] It is often seen that bad husbands have very good wives: whether it be that it raiseth the price of their husband's kindness when it comes, or that the wives take a pride in their patience. But this never fails if the bad husbands were of their own choosing, against their friends' consent; for then they will be sure to make good their own folly.

IX. OF ENVY

There be none of the affections which have been noted to fascinate or bewitch, but love and envy. They both have[1] vehement wishes; they frame themselves readily into imaginations and suggestions; and they come[2] easily into the eye, especially upon the presence of the objects; which are the points that conduce to fascination,[3] if any such thing there be. We see likewise the Scripture calleth envy an "evil eye,"[4] and

9. Exhausted. 10. The goddess Calypso offered immortality to Ulysses if he would not return to Ithaca and his wife. 11. Consequently a man has a pretext for marrying whenever he so desires. 12. Thales, one of the Seven Sages of ancient Greece, excused himself to his mother for not marrying by asserting at first that he was too young, and afterwards, that he was too old. 1. Beget. 2. Mount into. Cf. n. 4. 3. The Latin reads: "All these things conduce to bewitching." 4. *Mark* vii, 21-23.

the astrologers call the evil influences [5] of the stars "evil aspects," [6] so that still there seemeth to be acknowledged, in the act of envy, an ejaculation [7] or irradiation of the eye. Nay some have been so curious [8] as to note that the times when the stroke or percussion of an envious eye doth most hurt are when the party envied is beheld in glory or triumph, for that sets an edge upon [9] envy: and besides, at such times the spirits of the person envied do come forth most into the outward parts, and so meet the blow.

But leaving these curiosities [10] (though not unworthy to be thought on in fit place), we will handle what persons are apt to envy others; what persons are most subject to be envied themselves; and what is the difference between public and private envy.

A man that hath no virtue in himself ever envieth virtue in others. For men's minds will either feed upon their own good [11] or upon others' evil; [12] and who wanteth the one will prey upon the other; [13] and whoso is out of hope to attain to another's virtue, will seek to come at even hand [14] by depressing another's fortune.

A man that is busy and inquisitive is commonly envious. For to know much of other men's matters cannot be because all that ado may concern [15] his own estate; therefore it must needs be that he taketh a kind of play-pleasure [16] in looking upon the fortunes of others. Neither can he that mindeth but his own business find much matter for envy. For envy is a gadding passion, and walketh the streets, and doth not keep home: *Non est curiosus, quin idem sit malevolus* [No one is a busybody without also being malevolent].

Men of noble birth are noted to be envious towards new men when they rise. For the distance [17] is altered, and it is like a deceit of the eye, that when others come on they think themselves go back.

Deformed persons and eunuchs and old men and bastards are envious. For he that cannot possibly mend his own case

5. Originally an ethereal fluid believed to flow from the stars and to influence men's actions; later, an emanation of occult power. 6. Situations of stars with respect to each other. 7. Emission. 8. Carefully observant. 9. Sharpens. 10. Small concerns. 11. Virtue. 12. Misfortune. 13. The man who lacks virtue will prey upon the misfortunes of his neighbor. 14. To make things even. 15. Because all that busyness about others' affairs may benefit. 16. The pleasure felt in seeing a play. 17. Distance of social rank.

will do what he can to impair another's, except[18] these defects light upon a very brave and heroical nature which thinketh to make his natural wants[19] part of his honor, in that[20] it should be said than an eunuch or a lame man did such great matters; affecting[21] the honor of a miracle; as it was[22] in Narses[23] the eunuch, and Agesilaus[24] and Tamberlanes,[25] that were lame men.

The same is the case of men that rise after calamities and misfortunes. For they are as men fallen out with the times, and think other men's harms a redemption of their own sufferings. 50

They that desire to excel in too many matters, out of levity and vain glory, are ever envious. For they cannot want work,[26] it being impossible but many in some one of those things should surpass them. Which was the character of Adrian[27] the Emperor, that mortally envied poets and painters and artificers, in works wherein he had a vein[28] to excel.

Lastly, near kinsfolks and fellows in office and those that have been bred together are more apt to envy their equals when they are raised. For it doth upbraid unto them their own fortunes, and pointeth at them, and cometh oftener into their remembrance, and incurreth[29] likewise more into the note of others; and envy ever redoubleth from speech and fame. Cain's envy was the more vile and malignant towards his brother Abel,[30] because when his sacrifice was better accepted, there was no body to look on. Thus much for those that are apt to envy. 60

Concerning those that are more or less subject to envy: First, persons of eminent virtue, when they are advanced, are less envied. For their fortune seemeth but due unto them, and no man envieth the payment of a debt, but rewards and liberality rather. Again, envy is ever joined with the comparing of a man's self, and where there is no comparison, no envy; and therefore kings are not envied but by kings. Nevertheless it is to be noted that unworthy persons are most envied at their first coming in, and afterwards overcome it 70

18. Unless. 19. Defects. 20. So that. 21. Striving for. 22. As was the case. 23. Roman general. He defeated the Goths, who had taken Rome, and governed Italy from 554 to 567. 24. King of Sparta, d. 361 B.C. 25. Tamerlane or Timour, d. 1405, Tatar conqueror of Asia as far as China. 26. Something for their envy to work upon. 27. Hadrian, d. 138, designed a temple and banished an architect for criticizing the plan. 28. Disposition. 29. Obtrudes itself. 30. Cf. *Genesis* iv, 1-15.

better; whereas contrariwise, persons of worth and merit are most envied when their fortune continueth long. For by that time, though their virtue be the same, yet it hath not the same luster, for fresh men grow up that darken it.

Persons of noble blood are less envied in their rising, for it seemeth but right done to their birth. Besides, there seemeth not much added to their fortune; and envy is as the sunbeams, that beat hotter upon a bank or steep rising ground than upon a flat. And for the same reason those that are advanced by degrees are less envied than those that are advanced suddenly and *per saltum* [at a bound].

Those that have joined with their honor great travels,[31] cares, or perils, are less subject to envy. For men think that they earn their honors hardly, and pity them sometimes; and pity ever healeth envy. Wherefore you shall observe that the more deep and sober sort of politic persons,[32] in their greatness, are ever bemoaning themselves, what a life they lead, chanting a *quanta patimur* [how many things we suffer!]. Not that they feel it so, but only to abate the edge of envy. But this is to be understood of business that is laid upon men, and not such as they call unto themselves. For nothing increaseth envy more than an unnecessary and ambitious engrossing of business. And nothing doth extinguish envy more than for a great person to preserve all other inferior officers in their full rights and pre-eminences of their places. For by that means there be so many screens between him and envy.

Above all, those are most subject to envy, which carry the greatness of their fortunes in an insolent and proud manner, being never well but while they are showing how great they are, either by outward pomp, or by triumphing over all opposition or competition; whereas wise men will rather do sacrifice to envy, in suffering themselves sometimes of purpose [33] to be crossed and overborne in things that do not much concern them. Notwithstanding, so much is true, that the carriage of greatness in a plain and open manner (so it be without arrogancy and vainglory) doth draw less envy than if it be in a more crafty and cunning fashion. For in that course a man doth but disavow fortune, and seemeth to be conscious of his own want in worth, and doth but teach others to envy him.

Lastly, to conclude this part: as we said in the beginning that the act of envy had somewhat in it of witchcraft, so there

31. Labors. 32. Persons in public office. 33. Purposely.

is no other cure of envy but the cure of witchcraft, and that is, to remove the "lot"[34] (as they call it) and to lay it upon another. For which purpose, the wiser sort of great persons bring in ever upon the stage somebody upon whom to derive[35] the envy that would come upon themselves; sometimes upon ministers and servants; sometimes upon colleagues and associates, and the like; and for that turn there are never wanting some persons of violent and undertaking[36] natures, who, so they may have power and business, will take it at any cost. 120

Now, to speak of public envy. There is yet some good in public envy, whereas in private there is none. For public envy is as an ostracism, that eclipseth men when they grow too great. And therefore it is a bridle also to great ones, to keep them within bounds. 130

This envy, being in the Latin word *invidia,* goeth in the modern languages by the name of *discontentment,* of which we shall speak in handling sedition. It is a disease in a state like to infection. For as infection spreadeth upon that which is sound, and tainteth it, so when envy is gotten once into a state, it traduceth even the best actions thereof, and turneth them into an ill odor. And therefore there is little won by intermingling of plausible[37] actions. For that doth argue but a weakness and fear of envy, which hurteth so much the more, as it is likewise usual in infections, which if you fear them, you call them upon you. 140

This public envy seemeth to beat chiefly upon principal officers or ministers, rather than upon kings and estates themselves. But this is a sure rule, that if the envy upon the minister be great, when the cause of it in him is small, or if the envy be general in a manner upon all the ministers of an estate, then the envy (though hidden) is truly upon the state itself. And so much of public envy or discontentment, and the difference thereof from private envy, which was handled in the first place. 150

We will add this in general, touching the affection of envy, that of all other affections it is the most importune and continual. For of other affections there is occasion given but now and then; and therefore it was well said, *Invidia festos dies non agit* [Envy keeps no holidays], for it is ever working upon some or other. And it is also noted that love and envy do make a man pine, which other affections do not, because

34. Spell. 35. Bring down. 36. Enterprising. 37. Laudable.

160 they are not so continual. It is also the vilest affection, and the most depraved, for which cause it is the proper attribute of the devil, who is called "the envious man, that soweth tares amongst the wheat by night"; as it always cometh to pass that envy worketh subtilly and in the dark, and to the prejudice of good things such as is the wheat.

X. OF LOVE

The stage is more beholding [1] to love than the life of man. For as to the stage, love is ever a matter of comedies and now and then of tragedies, but in life it doth much mischief, sometimes like a siren,[2] sometimes like a fury.[3] You may observe that amongst all the great and worthy persons (whereof the memory remaineth, either ancient or recent) there is not one that hath been transported to the mad degree of love: which shows that great spirits and great business do keep out this weak passion. You must except nevertheless Marcus Antonius,[4]
10 the half partner of the empire of Rome, and Appius Claudius, the decemvir and lawgiver; [5] whereof the former was indeed a voluptuous man and inordinate, but the latter was an austere and wise man: and therefore it seems (though rarely) that love can find entrance not only into an open heart but also into a heart well fortified, if watch be not kept. It is a poor saying of Epicurus,[6] *Satis magnum alter alteri theatrum sumus* [One may find in one's neighbor a theater large enough], as if man, made for the contemplation of heaven and all noble objects, should do nothing but kneel before a little
20 idol and make himself a subject, though not of the mouth (as beasts are), yet of the eye, which was given him for higher purposes. It is a strange thing to note the excess of this passion and how it braves [7] the nature and value of things, by this:

1. Indebted: love provides more pleasure in the theater than in real life. 2. The Sirens were winged women who lived on a rocky isle and lured mariners to destruction with sweet songs. 3. The Furies were snake-haired, winged, avenging goddesses who punished men for various crimes; hence a fury is a malignant, angry spirit. 4. Mark Antony loved Cleopatra. 5. Virginius, a commoner, killed his daughter to protect her from the "mad" love of Appius. B. confused Appius with a later lawgiver of the same name. 6. See I, n. 11. 7. Insultingly disregards.

that the speaking in perpetual hyperbole is comely in nothing but in love. Neither is it merely in the phrase; for, whereas it hath been well said that the arch-flatterer, with whom all the petty flatterers have intelligence, is a man's self, certainly the lover is more.[8] For there was never proud man thought so absurdly well of himself as the lover doth of the person loved; and therefore it was well said, "That it is impossible to love and to be wise." Neither doth this weakness appear to others only and not to the party loved, but to the loved most of all, except[9] the love be reciprocal. For it is a true rule that love is ever rewarded either with the reciprocal or with an inward and secret contempt. By how much the more men ought to beware of this passion which loseth not only other things but itself! As for the other losses, the poet's relation doth well figure them: that he that preferred Helena quitted the gifts of Juno and Pallas.[10] For whosoever esteemeth too much of amorous affection quitteth both riches and wisdom. This passion hath his floods in the very times of weakness, which are great prosperity and great adversity, though this latter hath been less observed: both which times kindle love and make it more fervent, and therefore show it to be the child of folly. They do best who, if they cannot but admit love, yet make it keep quarter,[11] and sever it wholly from their serious affairs and actions of life; for if it check[12] once with business, it troubleth men's fortunes and maketh men that they can no ways be true to their own ends. I know not how, but martial men are given to love. I think it is but as they are given to wine; for perils commonly ask to be paid in pleasures. There is in man's nature a secret inclination and motion towards love of others, which, if it be not spent upon some one or a few, doth naturally spread itself towards many, and maketh men become humane and charitable, as it is seen sometime in friars. Nuptial love maketh mankind, friendly love perfecteth it, but wanton love corrupteth and embaseth it.

8. I.e., one's lover flatters one even more than one flatters oneself. 9. Unless. 10. Appealed to by the goddesses Juno, Venus and Pallas Athena to decide which was the most beautiful, Paris picked Venus who offered him the most beautiful woman in the world (Helen of Troy). He rejected the proffers of the others. 11. Within proper limits. 12. Interfere.

XI. OF GREAT PLACE

Men in great place are thrice servants: servants of the sovereign or state, servants of fame, and servants of business; so as [1] they have no freedom, neither in their persons nor in their actions nor in their times. It is a strange desire, to seek power and to lose liberty; or to seek power over others and to lose power over a man's self. The rising unto place is laborious, and by pains men come to greater pains; and it is sometimes base, and by indignities [2] men come to dignities. The standing is slippery, and the regress is either a downfall or at least an eclipse, which is a melancholy thing. *Cum non sis qui fueris, non esse cur velis vivere* [When you are no longer what you have been, there is no longer reason for wishing to live]. Nay, retire men cannot when they would; neither will they when it were reason,[3] but are impatient of privateness,[4] even in old age and sickness, which require the shadow; [5] like old townsmen that will be still sitting at their street door though thereby they offer age to scorn. Certainly great persons had need to borrow other men's opinions to think themselves happy, for if they judge by their own feeling they cannot find it; but if they think with themselves what other men think of them and that other men would fain be as they are, then they are happy as it were by report, when perhaps they find the contrary within. For they are the first that find their own griefs, though they be the last that find their own faults. Certainly men in great fortunes are strangers to themselves, and while they are in the puzzle of business they have no time to tend their health either of body or mind. *Illi mors gravis incubat, qui notus nimis omnibus, ignotus moritur sibi* [Death presses heavily on the man who is known to all others but dies ignorant of himself]. In place there is license to do good and evil, whereof the latter is a curse; for in evil the best condition is not to will; the second, not to can.[6] But power to do good is the true and lawful end of aspiring. For good thoughts (though God accept them) yet towards men are little better than good dreams except they be put in act, and that cannot be

1. That. 2. Undignified acts. 3. Reasonable. 4. Private life. 5. The shade of retirement rather than the light of publicity. 6. Be able.

without power and place as the vantage and commanding ground. Merit and good works is the end of man's motion, and conscience [7] of the same is the accomplishment of man's rest. For if a man can be a partaker of God's theater,[8] he shall likewise be partaker of God's rest. *Et conversus Deus, ut aspiceret opera quae fecerunt manus suae, vidit quod omnia essent bona nimis* [And God, turning to look upon the works which his hands had made, saw that all were very good]; and then the sabbath. In the discharge of thy place set before thee the best examples, for imitation is a globe of precepts.[9] And after a time set before thee thine own example, and examine thyself strictly whether thou didst not better at first. Neglect not also the examples of those that have carried themselves ill in the same place; not to set off thyself by taxing [10] their memory, but to direct thyself what to avoid. Reform therefore without bravery [11] or scandal of former times and persons, but yet set it down to thyself as well to create good precedents as to follow them. Reduce things to the first institution and observe wherein and how they have degenerated, but yet ask counsel of both times: of the ancient time, what is best; and of the latter time, what is fittest. Seek to make thy course regular, that men may know beforehand what they may expect; but be not too positive and peremptory; and express thyself well [12] when thou digressest from thy rule. Preserve the right of thy place, but stir not questions of jurisdiction, and rather assume thy right in silence and *de facto* [by right of possession] than voice it with claims and challenges. Preserve likewise the rights of inferior places, and think it more honor to direct in chief than to be busy in all. Embrace and invite helps and advices touching the execution of thy place, and do not drive away such as bring thee information, as meddlers; but accept of them in good part. The vices of authority are chiefly four: delays, corruption, roughness and facility.[13] For delays: give easy access; keep times appointed; go through with that which is in hand, and interlace not business [14] but of necessity. For corruption: do not only bind thine own hands or thy servants'

7. Consciousness. 8. If a man can regard the spectacle (theater) of his accomplishments with the knowledge that they are good. Cf. *Genesis,* i, 31. 9. Is (as valuable as) a collection of rules for conduct. 10. Censuring. 11. Ostentation. 12. Explain well your reasons. 13. Being easily led to change opinions; complaisance. 14. Mix different matters of business.

hands from taking, but bind the hands of suitors from offering. For integrity used doth the one; but integrity professed, and with a manifest detestation of bribery, doth the other. And avoid not only the fault but the suspicion. Whoever is found variable and changeth manifestly without manifest cause, giveth suspicion of corruption. Therefore always when thou changest thine opinion or course, profess it plainly and declare it together with the reasons that move thee to change,
80 and do not think to steal it.[15] A servant or favorite, if he be inward,[16] and no other apparent cause of esteem, is commonly thought but a by-way to close corruption. For roughness: it is a needless cause of discontent: severity breedeth fear, but roughness breedeth hate. Even reproofs from authority ought to be grave and not taunting. As for facility: it is worse than bribery, for bribes come but now and then; but if importunity or idle respects lead a man, he shall never be without.[17] As Solomon saith, "To respect persons is not good, for such a man will transgress for a piece of bread." [18] It is most true that was
90 anciently spoken, "A place showeth the man." And it showeth some to the better and some to the worse. *Omnium consensu capax imperii, nisi imperasset* [Everyone would have thought him fit for empire, had he not been emperor], saith Tacitus [19] of Galba; [20] but of Vespasian he saith, *Solus imperantium, Vespasianus mutatus in melius* [Vespasian was the only emperor whom the possession of power changed for the better]; though the one was meant of sufficiency,[21] the other of manners and affection.[22] It is an assured sign of a worthy and generous spirit whom honor amends,[23] for honor
100 is or should be the place [24] of virtue; and as in nature things move violently to their place and calmly in their place, so virtue in ambition is violent, in authority settled and calm. All rising to great place is by a winding stair; and if there be factions, it is good to side a man's self whilst he is in the rising, and to balance himself when he is placed. Use the memory of thy predecessor fairly and tenderly; for if thou dost not, it is a

15. Do it by stealth. 16. Intimate, "on the inside." 17. If trivial preferences influence a man, he will never rise above them. 18. To discriminate between individuals on personal grounds is bad; for such a man is the kind who will transgress for a trivial cause. 19. Roman historian. 20. Roman emperor. 21. Administrative ability. 22. Conduct and disposition. 23. If the pursuit of honor leads a man to amend his faults. 24. The point of reference for the exercise of virtue.

debt will sure be paid when thou art gone. If thou have colleagues, respect them, and rather call them when they look not for it than exclude them when they have reason to look to be called. Be not too sensible or too remembering of thy place in conversation and private answers to suitors, but let it rather be said, "When he sits in place, he is another man."

XII. OF BOLDNESS

It[1] is a trivial grammar-school text, but yet worthy a wise man's consideration: Question was asked of Demosthenes,[2] *what was the chief part of an orator?* He answered, "Action!"[3] *What next?* "Action!" *What next again?* "Action!" He said it that knew it best, and had by nature himself no advantage[4] in that he commended. A strange thing that that part of an orator which is but superficial and rather the virtue of a player should be placed so high above those other noble parts of invention, elocution and the rest—nay, almost alone, as if it were all in all! But the reason is plain. There is in human nature generally more of the fool than of the wise; and therefore those faculties by which the foolish part of men's minds is taken are most potent. Wonderful like is the case of boldness in civil business: *What first?* Boldness! *What second and third?* Boldness! And yet boldness is a child of ignorance and baseness, far inferior to other parts. But nevertheless it doth fascinate and bind hand and foot those that are either shallow in judgment or weak in courage, which are the greatest part; yea and prevaileth with wise men at weak times. Therefore we see it hath done wonders in popular[5] states, but with senates and princes less; and more ever upon the first entrance of bold persons into action than soon after, for boldness is an ill keeper of promise. Surely as there are mountebanks[6] for the natural body, so are there mountebanks for the politic body: men that undertake great cures and perhaps have been lucky in two or three experiments but want the grounds[7] of science and therefore cannot hold out. Nay you

1. The following story. 2. Greek orator, d. 322 B.C. 3. Gesticulation. 4. Demosthenes had to overcome a speech impediment. 5. Democratic. 6. Quack doctors. 7. Lack the basic principles.

shall see a bold fellow many times do Mahomet's miracle. Mahomet made the people believe that he would call an hill
30 to him and from the top of it offer up his prayers for the observers of his law. The people assembled; Mahomet called the hill to come to him, again and again; and when the hill stood still, he was never a whit abashed but said, "If the hill will not come to Mahomet, Mahomet will go to the hill." So these men, when they have promised great matters and failed most shamefully, yet (if they have the perfection of boldness) they will but slight it over, and make a turn,[8] and no more ado. Certainly to men of great judgment, bold persons are a sport to behold; nay and to the vulgar also, boldness has somewhat
40 of the ridiculous. For if absurdity be the subject of laughter, doubt you not but great boldness is seldom without some absurdity. Especially it is a sport to see, when a bold fellow is out of countenance, for that puts his face into a most shrunken and wooden posture; as needs it must, for in bashfulness the spirits do a little go and come; but with bold men upon like occasion, they stand at stay, like stale at chess, where it is no mate but yet the game cannot stir.[9] But this last were fitter for a satire than for a serious observation. This is well to be weighed, that boldness is ever blind: for it seeth not dangers
50 and inconveniences. Therefore it is ill in counsel, good in execution; so that the right use of bold persons is that they never command in chief but be seconds and under the direction of others. For in counsel it is good to see dangers, and in execution not to see them, except they be very great.

XIII. OF GOODNESS AND GOODNESS OF NATURE

I take goodness in this sense, the affecting[1] of the weal of men, which is that the Grecians call *philanthropia;* and the word *humanity* (as it is used) is a little too light to express it. Goodness I call the habit, and goodness of nature the inclina-

8. Reverse their position. 9. The expressions of shy men keep changing according to their changed feelings, but when bold men are abashed, their expressions are immobilized or stalemated as in chess; for in such a fix, any motion means defeat. 1. Desiring.

tion. This of all virtues and dignities of the mind is the greatest, being the character[2] of the Deity, and without it man is a busy,[3] mischievous, wretched thing, no better than a kind of vermin. Goodness answers to the theological virtue charity, and admits no excess but error. The desire of power in excess caused the angels to fall; the desire of knowledge in excess caused man to fall: but in charity there is no excess; neither can angel or man come in danger by it. The inclination to goodness is imprinted deeply in the nature of man, insomuch that if it issue not towards men, it will take unto other living creatures, as it is seen in the Turks, a cruel people, who nevertheless are kind to beasts and give alms to dogs and birds; insomuch as Busbechius[4] reporteth, a Christian boy in Constantinople had like to have been stoned for gagging in a waggishness a long-billed fowl. Errors indeed in this virtue of goodness or charity may be committed. The Italians have an ungracious proverb, *Tanto buon che val niente* [So good, that he is good for nothing]. And one of the doctors[5] of Italy, Nicholas Machiavel, had the confidence to put in writing, almost in plain terms, "That the Christian faith had given up good men in prey to those that are tyrannical and unjust"; which he spake, because indeed there was never law or sect or opinion did so much magnify goodness as the Christian religion doth. Therefore, to avoid the scandal and the danger both, it is good to take knowledge of the errors of an habit so excellent. Seek the good of other men, but be not in bondage to their faces or fancies, for that is but facility or softness, which taketh an honest mind prisoner. Neither give thou Æsop's[6] cock a gem, who would be better pleased and happier if he had had a barley-corn. The example of God teacheth the lesson truly: "He sendeth his rain and maketh his sun to shine upon the just and unjust";[7] but he doth not rain wealth, nor shine honor and virtues upon men equally. Common benefits are to be communicate with all, but peculiar benefits with choice. And beware how in making the portraiture thou breakest the pattern. For divinity maketh the love of ourselves the pattern; the love of our neighbors but the

2. Attribute. 3. Restless. 4. 16th century Flemish scholar and ambassador to Turkey. 5. Teachers. In *Discourses on Livy,* Nicholas Machiavelli, d. 1527, says that emphasis on humility and unworldliness make Christians prey to injustice; however, he adds that such a view of Christian teaching is erroneous—a qualification which Bacon passes over. 6. Writer of fables, ca. 560 B.C. 7. *Matthew* v, 5.

portraiture. "Sell all thou hast, and give it to the poor, and follow me," but sell not all thou hast, except thou come and follow me; that is, except thou have a vocation wherein thou mayest do as much good with little means as with great, for otherwise in feeding the streams thou driest the fountain. Neither is there only a habit of goodness, directed by right reason; but there is in some men, even in nature, a disposition towards it, as on the other side there is a natural malignity.
50 For there be that in their nature do not affect[8] the good of others. The lighter sort of malignity turneth but to a crossness or frowardness or aptness to oppose or difficilness[9] or the like; but the deeper sort, to envy and mere mischief. Such men in other men's calamities are, as it were, in season, and are ever on the loading part: not so good as the dogs that licked Lazarus'[10] sores; but like flies that are still buzzing upon any thing that is raw, *misanthropi* [haters of men], that make it their practice to bring men to the bough, and yet have never a tree for the purpose in their gardens, as Timon[11] had. Such
60 dispositions are the very errors of human nature, and yet they are the fittest timber to make great politics[12] of; like to knee[13] timber, that is good for ships, that are ordained to be tossed; but not for building houses, that shall stand firm. The parts and signs of goodness are many. If a man be gracious and courteous to strangers, it shows he is a citizen of the world, and that his heart is no island cut off from other lands, but a continent that joins to them. If he be compassionate towards the afflictions of others, it shows that his heart is like the noble tree that is wounded itself when it gives the balm.[14] If he easily
70 pardons and remits offences, it shows that his mind is planted above injuries, so that he cannot be shot. If he be thankful for small benefits, it shows that he weighs men's minds and not their trash. But above all, if he have St. Paul's perfection, that he would wish to be an *anathema* from Christ for the salvation of his brethren,[15] it shows much of a divine nature, and a kind of conformity with Christ himself.

8. Desire. 9. Hardness to deal with. 10. Beggar in a parable, *Luke*, xvi, 21. 11. Timon, surnamed the Misanthrope, publicly announced that since he was going to cut down a tree upon which many had hanged themselves, would-be suicides should use it at once; i.e., he openly professed his hatred of men. 12. Politicians. 13. Crooked. 14. When wounded, the frankincense tree exudes aromatic resin. 15. To be accursed by Christ if such a curse could save his fellow Jews; i.e., Paul was willing to suffer for the good of others.

XIV. OF NOBILITY

We will speak of nobility first as a portion of an estate;[1] then as a condition of particular persons. A monarchy where there is no nobility at all is ever a pure and absolute tyranny, as that of the Turks; for nobility attempers sovereignty and draws the eyes of the people somewhat aside from the line royal. But for democracies, they need it not; and they are commonly more quiet and less subject to sedition than where there are stirps [2] of nobles—for men's eyes are upon the business and not upon the persons; or, if upon the persons, it is for the business' sake, as fittest, and not for flags and pedigree. We see the Switzers last well, notwithstanding their diversity of religion and of cantons; for utility is their bond, and not respects.[3] The United Provinces of the Low Countries in their government excel; for where there is an equality, the consultations are more indifferent,[4] and the payments and tributes more cheerful. A great and potent nobility addeth majesty to a monarch, but diminisheth power; and putteth life and spirit into the people, but presseth their fortune. It is well when nobles are not too great for sovereignty nor for justice, and yet maintained in that height as [5] the insolency of inferiors may be broken upon them before it come on too fast upon the majesty of kings. A numerous nobility causeth poverty and inconvenience in a state, for it is a surcharge of expense; and besides, it being of necessity that many of the nobility fall in time to be weak in fortune, it maketh a kind of disproportion between honor and means.

As for nobility in particular persons, it is a reverend thing to see an ancient castle or building not in decay, or to see a fair timber tree sound and perfect. How much more to behold an ancient noble family which hath stood against the waves and weathers of time! For new nobility is but the act of power, but ancient nobility is the act of time. Those that are first raised to nobility are commonly more virtuous but less innocent than their descendants—for there is rarely any rising but by a commixture of good and evil arts. But it is reason [6] the memory of their virtues remain to their posterity, and their faults die with

1. A state. 2. Families. 3. Considerations for rank. 4. Impartial. 5. In such a height that. 6. It is reasonable that.

themselves. Nobility of birth commonly abateth industry, and he that is not industrious envieth him that is: besides, noble persons cannot go much higher; and he that standeth at a stay[7] when others rise can hardly avoid motions[8] of envy. On the other side, nobility extinguisheth the passive envy from others towards them because they are in possession of honor.[9] Certainly, kings that have able men of their nobility, shall find ease in employing them, and a better slide into their business; for people naturally bend to them as born in some sort to command.

XVI. OF ATHEISM

I had rather believe all the fables in the Legend,[1] and the Talmud[2] and the Alcoran[3] than that this universal frame is without a mind. And therefore God never wrought miracle to convince[4] atheism, because his ordinary works convince it. It is true that a little philosophy inclineth man's mind to atheism, but depth in philosophy bringeth men's minds about to religion. For while the mind of man looketh upon second causes scattered, it may sometimes rest in them, and go no further; but when it beholdeth the chain of them, confederate and linked together, it must needs fly to Providence and Deity.[5] Nay, even that school which is most accused of atheism doth most demonstrate religion;[6] that is, the school of Leucippus and Democritus and Epicurus.[7] For it is a thousand times

7. Standstill. 8. Impulses. 9. A comparison with the Latin indicates B's meaning: If a man is born to a title, the latent envy which might arise against him in men of lesser rank is prevented from arising; but *active* envy flames up in a man who fails to rise, against those who are given such titles instead of being born to them. 1. 13th century collection of saints' lives by Jacobus de Voragine, which includes miraculous stories of saints walking with their heads off, etc. 2. Compilation of Jewish laws. 3. The Koran, sacred book of the Mohammedans. 4. Overcome. 5. If a man directs his mind only to immediate causes of things and phenomena without seeing how they are related, he may be content to think no further. But if he sees that there is a chain of causes whereby A is caused by B; B by C; C by D, and so on, then he will follow the chain back until he comes to the First Cause, Providence or God. 6. Even the group of thinkers who taught that the physical universe was formed of atoms coming together by chance (not by the will of a Creator) demonstrate the truth of religion, although they are accused of atheism. 7. Atomic philosophers of the 5th and 4th centuries B.C.

more credible that four mutable elements and one immutable fifth essence,[8] duly and eternally placed, need no God, than that an army of infinite small portions or seeds[9] unplaced, should have produced this order and beauty without a divine marshal.[10] The Scripture saith, "The fool hath said in his heart, there is no God"; it is not said, "The fool hath thought in his heart"; so as he rather saith it by rote to himself, as that[11] he would have, than that he can thoroughly believe it or be persuaded of it. For none deny there is a God but those for whom it maketh[12] that there were no God. It appeareth in nothing more, that atheism is rather in the lip than in the heart of man, than by this: that atheists will ever be talking of that their opinion, as if they fainted in it within themselves and would be glad to be strengthened by the consent of others. Nay more, you shall have atheists strive to get disciples, as it fareth with other sects. And, which is most of all, you shall have of them that will suffer for atheism and not recant; whereas if they did truly think that there were no such thing as God, why should they trouble themselves? Epicurus is charged that he did but dissemble for his credit's sake when he affirmed there were blessed natures, but such as enjoyed themselves without having respect to the government of the world. Wherein they say he did temporize, though in secret he thought there was no God. But certainly he is traduced; for his words are noble and divine: *Non deos vulgi negare profanum; sed vulgi opiniones diis applicare profanum* [It is not profane to repudiate the gods of the vulgar, but it is profane to attach to the gods vulgar conceptions of them]. Plato could have said no more. And although he had the confidence to deny the administration, he had not the power to deny the nature. The Indians of the West have names for their particular gods, though they have no name for God: as if the heathens should have had the names Jupiter, Apollo, Mars, etc. but not the word *Deus;*[13] which shows that even those barbarous people have the notion, though they have not the latitude and extent of it. So that against atheists the very

8. In opposition to the atomic theory, Aristotle and later thinkers taught that our earth was composed of four changeable elements—earth, air, fire and water—and that the rest of the physical universe was made of an unchangeable fifth element or essence. 9. Atoms. 10. Without a God to give them order. 11. That which. 12. Seems advantageous to believe. 13. God.

savages take part with the very subtlest philosophers. The contemplative atheist is rare: a Diagoras,[14] a Bion,[15] a Lucian[16] perhaps, and some others; and yet they seem to be more than they are, for that all that impugn a received religion or superstition are by the adverse part branded with the name of atheists. But the great atheists indeed are hypocrites, which are ever handling holy things, but without feeling; so as they must needs be cauterized in the end. The causes of atheism are divisions in religion, if they be many, for any one main division addeth zeal to both sides, but many divisions introduce atheism. Another is scandal of priests, when it is come to that which St. Bernard[17] saith, *Non est jam dicere, ut populus sic sacerdos; quia nec sic populus ut sacerdos* ['As the people are, so is the priest' may no longer be said, but rather, 'As the people are, so the priest is not' (for they are better than he).] A third is custom of profane scoffing in holy matters, which doth by little and little deface the reverence of religion. And lastly, learned times, specially with peace and prosperity, for troubles and adversities do more bow men's minds to religion. They that deny a God destroy man's nobility, for certainly man is of kin to the beasts by his body, and if he be not of kin to God by his spirit, he is a base and ignoble creature. It destroys likewise magnanimity, and the raising of human nature; for take an example of a dog and mark what a generosity and courage he will put on when he finds himself maintained by a man, who to him is instead of a God or *melior natura* [better nature]; which courage is manifestly such as that creature, without that confidence of a better nature than his own, could never attain. So man, when he resteth and assureth himself upon divine protection and favor, gathereth a force and faith which human nature in itself could not obtain. Therefore, as atheism is in all respects hateful, so in this, that it depriveth human nature of the means to exalt itself above human frailty. As it is in particular persons, so it is in nations. Never was there such a state for magnanimity as Rome. Of this state hear what Cicero saith: *Quam volumus licet, patres conscripti, nos amemus, tamen nec numero Hispanos, nec robore Gallos, nec calliditate Pœnos, nec artibus Græcos, nec denique hoc ipso hujus gentis*

14. 5th century Greek poet, outlawed from Athens for his avowed atheism. 15. Philosopher, 3rd century B.C. 16. Greek satirist, 2nd century. 17. French abbot, 12th century.

et terræ domestico nativoque sensu Italos ipsos et Latinos; sed pietate, ac religione, atque hac una sapientia, quod deorum immortalium numine omnia regi gubernarique perspeximus, omnes gentes nationesque superavimus. [We may admire ourselves, Conscript Fathers, as much as we please; yet we cannot match the Spaniards in number, the Gauls in bodily strength, the Carthaginians in craft, the Greeks in art, nor our own Italians and Latins in the homebred and native good sense characteristic of this land and nation. But our piety, our religion, and our recognition of the one great truth that all things are regulated and governed by the providence of the immortal gods—these are the points in which we have surpassed all the tribes and nations of the world].

XVII. OF SUPERSTITION

It were better to have no opinion of God at all, than such an opinion as is unworthy of him. For the one is unbelief, the other is contumely; and certainly superstition is the reproach of the Deity. Plutarch[1] saith well to that purpose: "Surely," saith he, "I had rather a great deal men should say there was no such man at all as Plutarch, than that they should say that there was one Plutarch that would eat his children as soon as they were born"; as the poets speak of Saturn.[2] And as the contumely is greater towards God, so the danger is greater towards men. Atheism leaves a man to sense, to philosophy, to natural piety, to laws, to reputation; all which may be guides to an outward moral virtue, though religion were not; but superstition dismounts all these and erecteth an absolute monarchy in the minds of men. Therefore atheism did never perturb states, for it makes men wary of themselves, as looking no further; and we see the times inclined to atheism (as the time of Augustus Cæsar[3]) were civil times. But superstition hath been the confusion of many states and bringeth in a new *primum mobile*[4] that ravisheth all the spheres of gov-

1. Greek biographer and moralist, d. 120. 2. Roman equivalent of Chronos in Greek mythology. He devoured his children, except Zeus, for whom a stone was substituted. 3. Roman emperor, d. 14. 4. See I, n. 14.

20 ernment. The master of superstition is the people, and in all superstition wise men follow fools, and arguments are fitted to practice, in a reversed order. It was gravely said by some of the prelates in the Council of Trent,[5] where the doctrine of the Schoolmen [6] bare great sway, "that the Schoolmen were like astronomers, which did feign eccentrics and epicycles, and such engines of orbs, to save the phenomena,[7] though they knew there were no such things"; and in like manner, that the Schoolmen had framed a number of subtle and intricate axioms and theorems to save the practice of the church. 30 The causes of superstition are: pleasing and sensual [8] rites and ceremonies; excess of outward and pharisaical holiness; overgreat reverence of traditions which cannot but load the church; the stratagems of prelates for their own ambition and lucre; the favoring too much of good intentions, which openeth the gate to conceits and novelties; the taking an aim at divine matters by human, which cannot but breed mixture of imaginations: [9] and, lastly, barbarous times, especially joined with calamities and disasters. Superstition without a veil is a deformed thing, for as it addeth deformity to an ape 40 to be so like a man, so the similitude of superstition to religion makes it the more deformed. And as wholesome meat corrupteth to little worms, so good forms and orders corrupt into a number of petty observances. There is a superstition in avoiding superstition, when men think to do best if they go furthest from the superstition formerly received; therefore care would be had that (as it fareth in ill purgings) the good be not taken away with the bad, which commonly is done when the people is the reformer.

5. Religious conference, 1545-63, convened to oppose Protestant doctrines and to settle disputed Roman Catholic ones. 6. Medieval philosophers whose aim was a logical treatment of religious dogma in conformity with reason and their interpretation of Aristotle's philosophy. They systematized thought so subtly that their scholasticism impeded scientific progress. 7. In order to reconcile Ptolemaic astronomy with newly observed phenomena, astronomers pretended that planets moved in eccentric orbits or in circles centered on them (epicycles). 8. Sensuous. 9. Conceptions. B. insisted that science and religion were to be kept in separate departments.

XVIII. OF TRAVEL

Travel in the younger sort is a part of education; in the elder, a part of experience. He that traveleth into a country before he hath some entrance into the language goeth to school and not to travel. That young men travel under some tutor or grave servant, I allow [1] well; so that he be such a one that hath the language, and hath been in the country before, whereby he may be able to tell them what things are worthy to be seen in the country where they go, what acquaintances they are to seek, what exercises or discipline [2] the place yieldeth. For else young men shall go hooded,[3] and look abroad little. It is a strange thing that in sea voyages, where there is nothing to be seen but sky and sea, men should make diaries; but in land-travel, wherein so much is to be observed, for the most part they omit it; as if chance were fitter to be registered than observation. Let diaries therefore be brought in use. The things to be seen and observed are: the courts of princes, specially when they give audience to ambassadors; the courts of justice, while they sit and hear causes, and so of consistories ecclesiastic; the churches and monasteries, with the monuments which are therein extant; the walls and fortifications of cities and towns, and so the havens and harbors; antiquities and ruins; libraries, colleges, disputations,[4] and lectures, where any are; shipping and navies; houses and gardens of state and pleasure near great cities; armories; arsenals; magazines; [5] exchanges; burses; [6] warehouses; exercises of horsemanship, fencing, training of soldiers, and the like; comedies, such whereunto the better sort of persons do resort; treasuries of jewels and robes; cabinets and rarities; and, to conclude, whatsoever is memorable in the places where they go. After all which the tutors or servants ought to make diligent inquiry. As for triumphs, masks, feasts, weddings, funerals, capital executions, and such shows, men need not to be put in mind of them; yet are they not to be neglected. If you will have a young man to put his travel into a little room, and in short

1. Approve. 2. Learning. 3. In falconry, the head of a hawk is kept covered by a hood which prevents it from seeing anything. 4. Academic debates usually on philosophical subjects as used in the curricula of universities. 5. Storehouses. 6. Money markets.

time to gather much, this you must do. First, as was said, he must have some entrance into the language before he goeth. Then he must have such a servant or tutor as knoweth the country, as was likewise said. Let him carry with him also some card[7] or book describing the country where he travel-
40 eth, which will be a good key to his inquiry. Let him keep also a diary. Let him not stay long in one city or town; more or less as the place deserveth, but not long; nay, when he stayeth in one city or town, let him change his lodging from one end and part of the town to another, which is a great adamant[8] of acquaintance. Let him sequester himself from the company of his countrymen, and diet in such places where there is good company of the nation where he traveleth. Let him upon his removes from one place to another procure recommendation to some person of quality residing in the
50 place whither he removeth, that he may use his favor in those things he desireth to see or know. Thus he may abridge his travel with much profit. As for the acquaintance which is to be sought in travel, that which is most of all profitable is acquaintance with the secretaries and employed men of ambassadors, for so in traveling in one country he shall suck the experience of many. Let him also see and visit eminent persons in all kinds which are of great name abroad, that he may be able to tell how the life agreeth with the fame. For quarrels, they are with care and discretion to be avoided. They are
60 commonly for mistresses, healths, place, and words. And let a man beware how he keepeth company with choleric and quarrelsome persons, for they will engage him into their own quarrels. When a traveler returneth home, let him not leave the countries where he hath traveled altogether behind him, but maintain a correspondence by letters with those of his acquaintance which are of most worth. And let his travel appear rather in his discourse than in his apparel or gesture, and in his discourse let him be rather advised in his answers than forwards to tell stories, and let it appear that he doth not
70 change his country manners[9] for those of foreign parts, but only prick in some flowers of that he hath learned abroad into the customs of his own country.

7. Chart or map. 8. Loadstone or naturally magnetic iron oxide; hence, attractor. 9. Manners of his own country.

XXI. OF DELAYS

Fortune is like the market; where many times, if you can stay a little, the price will fall. And again, it is sometimes like Sibylla's [1] offer, which at first offereth the commodity at full, then consumeth part and part, and still holdeth up the price. For occasion [2] (as it is in the common verse) "turneth a bald noddle, after she hath presented her locks in front, and no hold taken"; or at least turneth the handle of the bottle first to be received, and after the belly, which is hard to clasp. There is surely no greater wisdom than well to time the beginnings and onsets of things. Dangers are no more light, if they once seem light; and more dangers have deceived men than forced them. Nay, it were better to meet some dangers half way, though they come nothing near, than to keep too long a watch upon their approaches; for if a man watch too long, it is odds he will fall asleep. On the other side, to be deceived with too long shadows (as some have been when the moon was low and shone on their enemies' back), and so to shoot off before the time, or to teach dangers to come on, by over early buckling [3] towards them, is another extreme. The ripeness or unripeness of the occasion (as we said) must ever be well weighed; and generally it is good to commit the beginnings of all great actions to Argus [4] with his hundred eyes, and the ends to Briareus [5] with his hundred hands, first to watch, and then to speed. For the helmet of Pluto,[6] which maketh the politic man go invisible, is secrecy in the counsel and celerity in the execution. For when things are once come to the execution, there is no secrecy comparable to celerity, like the motion of a bullet in the air, which flieth so swift as it outruns the eye.

1. Sibyl, a prophetess, offered to sell nine books to Tarquin, the Roman king. When he refused, she destroyed three but demanded the same price for the rest. Again he declined, and she burned three more, asking the original price for the remainder. They were bought and found to contain political and religious information. In times of crisis, the Romans consulted these Sybilline books. 2. Opportunity. Cf. "Seize time by the forelock." 3. Hurrying. 4. Greek mythological monster with one hundred eyes. He guarded Io after Zeus turned her into a cow. 5. A Titan, son of Gaea, Earth, and Uranus, Heaven. 6. God of the lower world; his helmet made its wearer invisible.

XXII. OF CUNNING

We take cunning for a sinister or crooked wisdom. And certainly there is a great difference between a cunning man and a wise man, not only in point of honesty, but in point of ability. There be that can pack the cards, and yet cannot play well; so there are some that are good in canvasses and factions, that are otherwise weak men. Again, it is one thing to understand persons, and another thing to understand matters, for many are perfect in men's humors, that are not greatly capable of the real part of business, which is the constitution of one
10 that hath studied men more than books. Such men are fitter for practice [1] than for counsel, and they are good but in their own alley: [2] turn them to new men, and they have lost their aim; so as the old rule to know a fool from a wise man, *Mitte ambos nudos ad ignotos, et videbis* [Send them both naked among strangers, and then you will see], doth scarce hold for them. And because these cunning men are like haberdashers of small wares, it is not amiss to set forth their shop.

It is a point of cunning, to wait upon [3] him with whom you speak, with your eye, as the Jesuits give it in precept, for there
20 be many wise men that have secret hearts and transparent countenances. Yet this would be done with a demure abasing of your eye sometimes, as the Jesuits also do use.

Another is that when you have anything to obtain of present despatch, you entertain and amuse the party with whom you deal with some other discourse, that he be not too much awake to make objections. I knew a counsellor and secretary that never came to Queen Elizabeth of England with bills to sign, but he would always first put her into some discourse of estate,[4] that she mought [5] the less mind the bills.

30 The like surprise may be made by moving [6] things when the party is in haste and cannot stay to consider advisedly of that is moved.

If a man would cross [7] a business that he doubts [8] some other would handsomely and effectually move, let him pretend to wish it well, and move it himself in such sort as may foil it.

The breaking off in the midst of that one was about to say,

1. Plotting. 2. Bowling-alley. 3. To watch carefully. 4. State affairs. 5. Might. 6. Proposing. 7. Prevent. 8. Suspects.

nothing doth more hurt in a state than that cunning men pass for wise.

But certainly some there are that know the resorts and falls [18] of business, that cannot sink into the main of it, like a house that hath convenient stairs and entries but never a fair room. Therefore you shall see them find out pretty looses [19] in the conclusion, but are no ways able to examine or debate matters. And yet commonly they take advantage of their inability and would be thought wits of direction. Some 120 build rather upon the abusing of others, and (as we now say) "putting tricks upon them," than upon soundness of their own proceedings. But Solomon saith, *Prudens advertit ad gressus suos; stultus divertit ad dolos* [The wisdom of the prudent is to understand his way, but the folly of fools is deceit].

XXIII. OF WISDOM FOR A MAN'S SELF

An ant is a wise creature for itself, but it is a shrewd [1] thing in an orchard or garden. And certainly men that are great lovers of themselves waste the public. Divide with reason between self-love and society, and be so true to thyself, as thou be not false to others, specially to thy king and country. It is a poor center of a man's actions, *himself*. It is right earth, for that only stands fast upon his own center, whereas all things that have affinity with the heavens move upon the center of another, which they benefit.[2] The referring of all to a man's self is more tolerable in a sovereign prince, because themselves 10 are not only themselves, but their good and evil is at the peril of the public fortune. But it is a desperate evil in a servant to a prince, or a citizen in a republic. For whatsoever affairs pass such a man's hands, he crooketh them to his own ends; which must needs be often eccentric to [3] the ends of his master or state. Therefore let princes or states choose such servants as have not this mark, except they mean their service should be

18. Ups and downs. 19. Shots of an arrow. Sometimes they will make what proves to be a lucky shot. 1. Mischievous. 2. It is just like the earth, for it alone, according to Ptolemaic astronomy, remains stationary. 3. Without the same center as; different from.

made but the accessory.[4] That which maketh the effect more pernicious is that all proportion is lost. It were disproportion
20 enough for the servant's good to be preferred before the master's, but yet it is a greater extreme when a little good of the servant shall carry things against a great good of the master's. And yet that is the case of bad officers, treasurers, ambassadors, generals, and other false and corrupt servants, which set a bias upon their bowl,[5] of [6] their own petty ends and envies, to the overthrow of their master's great and important affairs. And for the most part, the good such servants receive is after the model of their own fortune, but the hurt they sell for that good is after the model of their master's fortune. And certainly
30 it is the nature of extreme self-lovers, as they will set an house on fire, and [7] it were but to roast their eggs, and yet these men many times hold credit with their masters, because their study is but to please them and profit themselves; and for either respect they will abandon the good of their affairs.

Wisdom for a man's self is, in many branches thereof, a depraved thing. It is the wisdom of rats, that will be sure to leave a house somewhat before it fall. It is the wisdom of the fox, that thrusts out the badger, who digged and made room for him. It is the wisdom of crocodiles, that shed tears when
40 they would devour. But that which is specially to be noted is, that those which (as Cicero says of Pompey) are *sui amantes, sine rivali* [lovers of themselves without a rival] are many times unfortunate. And whereas they have all their times sacrificed to themselves, they become in the end themselves sacrifices to the inconstancy of fortune, whose wings they thought by their self-wisdom to have pinioned.

4. Secondary interest. 5. Are diverted from their proper duties. If a weight or bias is inserted in one side of a ball in bowling, it is deflected from its proper course. 6. (A bias in favor) of. 7. Even if.

XXIV. OF INNOVATIONS

As the births of living creatures at first are ill-shapen, so are all innovations, which are the births of time. Yet notwithstanding, as those that first bring honor into their family are commonly more worthy than most that succeed, so the first precedent (if it be good) is seldom attained by imitation. For ill, to man's nature as it stands perverted, hath a natural motion, strongest in continuance; but good, as a forced motion, strongest at first.[1] Surely every medicine is an innovation, and he that will not apply new remedies must expect new evils, for time is the greatest innovator, and if time of course [2] alter things to the worse, and wisdom and counsel shall not alter them to the better, what shall be the end? It is true, that what is settled by custom, though it be not good, yet at least it is fit; and those things which have long gone together are as it were confederate within themselves; whereas new things piece not so well, but though they help by their utility, yet they trouble by their inconformity. Besides, they are like strangers, more admired [3] and less favored. All this is true, if time stood still, which contrariwise moveth so round [4] that a froward retention of custom is as turbulent a thing as an innovation; and they that reverence too much old times are but a scorn to the new. It were good therefore that men in their innovations would follow the example of time itself, which indeed innovateth greatly, but quietly, and by degrees scarce to be perceived. For otherwise, whatsoever is new is unlooked for, and ever it mends some, and pairs [5] other; and he that is holpen takes it for a fortune [6] and thanks the time; and he that is hurt, for a wrong, and imputeth it to the author. It is good also not to try experiments in states, except the necessity be urgent or the utility evident; and well to beware that it be the reformation that draweth on the change, and not the desire of change

1. I.e., man is naturally depraved, and evil therefore grows greater naturally in him; but goodness is contrary to his fallen nature and has to be imposed upon it. Accordingly, goodness tends naturally to diminish. For example, if a naturally lazy man forces himself to work, he finds it easier to decrease rather than to maintain his industriousness. 2. If in the course of time. 3. Regarded with curiosity. 4. Swiftly. 5. Impairs. 6. Good luck.

that pretendeth [7] the reformation; and lastly, that the novelty, though it be not rejected, yet be held for a suspect, and, as the Scripture saith, "that we make a stand upon the ancient way, and then look about us, and discover what is the straight and right way, and so to walk in it."

XXV. OF DISPATCH

Affected dispatch [1] is one of the most dangerous things to business that can be: it is like that which the physicians call *predigestion,* or hasty digestion, which is sure to fill the body full of crudities and secret seeds of diseases; therefore, measure not dispatch by the times of sitting but by the advancement of the business: and as in races it is not the large stride, or high lift that makes the speed, so in business the keeping close to the matter and not taking of it too much at once, procureth dispatch. It is the care of some, only to come off speedily for 10 the time, or to contrive some false periods of business, because [2] they may seem men of dispatch: but it is one thing to abbreviate by contracting; another, by cutting off. And business so handled at several sittings or meetings goeth commonly backward and forward in an unsteady manner. I knew a wise man that had it for a by-word, when he saw men hasten to a conclusion, "Stay a little, that we may make an end the sooner."

On the other side, true dispatch is a rich thing; for time is the measure of business, as money is of wares; and business is 20 bought at a dear hand where there is small dispatch. The Spartans and Spaniards have been noted to be of small dispatch: *Mi venga la muerte de Spagna*: "Let my death come from Spain"; for then it will be sure to be long in coming.

Give good hearing to those that give the first information in business, and rather direct them in the beginning than interrupt them in the continuance of their speeches; for he that is put out of his own order will go forward and backward and be more tedious while he waits upon his memory, than he could have been if he had gone on his own course. But sometimes

7. Brings forward as an excuse. 1. An excessive desire for dispatch. 2. In order that.

it is seen that the moderator is more troublesome than the actor. 30

Iterations[3] are commonly loss of time; but there is no such gain of time as to iterate often the state of the question; for it chaseth away many a frivolous speech as it is coming forth. Long and curious[4] speeches are as fit for dispatch as a robe or mantle with a long train is for a race. Prefaces and passages[5] and excusations[6] and other speeches of reference to the person are great wastes of time; and though they seem to proceed of[7] modesty, they are bravery.[8] Yet beware of being too material[9] when there is any impediment or obstruction in men's wills; for pre-occupation of mind ever requireth preface of speech, like a fomentation to make the unguent enter. 40

Above all things, order and distribution and singling out of parts is the life of dispatch, so as[10] the distribution be not too subtle; for he that doth not divide will never enter well into business, and he that divideth too much will never come out of it clearly. To choose time is to save time, and an unseasonable motion is but beating the air. There be three parts of business—the preparation, the debate or examination, and the perfection,—whereof, if you look for dispatch, let the middle only be the work of many, and the first and last the work of few. The proceeding upon somewhat[11] conceived in writing doth for the most part facilitate dispatch; for though it should be wholly rejected, yet that negative is more pregnant of direction[12] than an indefinite, as ashes are more generative than dust. 50

XXVI. OF SEEMING WISE

It hath been an opinion, that the French are wiser than they seem, and the Spaniards, seem wiser than they are; but howsoever it be between nations, certainly it is so between man and man; for, as the Apostle saith of godliness, "Having a show of godliness, but denying the power thereof,"[1] so cer-

3. Repetitions. 4. Elaborate. 5. Transitions from one part of a speech to another. 6. Apologies. 7. From. 8. Mere ostentation. 9. Blunt; candid. 10. Provided that. 11. Something. 12. Rich in guidance (towards new plans); suggestive. 1. St. Paul, II *Timothy,* iii, 5.

tainly there are, in point of wisdom and sufficiency, that do nothing[2] or little, very solemnly: *magno conatu nugas.* [trifles with great effort]. It is a ridiculous thing, and fit for a satire to persons of judgment, to see what shifts these
10 formalists[3] have, and what prospectives to make *superficies* [surfaces] to seem body that hath depth and bulk.[4] Some are so close and reserved as[5] they will not show their wares but by a dark light and seem always to keep back somewhat; and when they know within themselves they speak of that[6] they do not well know, would nevertheless seem to others to know[7] of that which they may not well speak. Some help themselves with countenance and gesture and are wise by signs; as Cicero saith of Piso, that when he answered him he fetched one of his brows up to his forehead and bent the
20 other down to his chin: *Respondes, altero ad frontem sublato, altero ad mentum depresso supercilio, crudelitatem tibi non placere* [You reply with one eyebrow hoisted to your forehead and the other bent down to your chin, that you do not approve of cruelty]. Some think to bear[8] it by speaking a great word, and being peremptory, and go on and take by admittance that which they cannot make good. Some, whatsoever is beyond their reach, will seem to despise or make light of it as impertinent or curious,[9] and so would have their ignorance seem judgment. Some are never without a difference,[10] and com-
30 monly by amusing men with a subtletly, blanch[11] the matter; of whom A. Gellius[12] saith, *Hominem delirum, qui verborum minutiis rerum frangit pondera.* [A senseless man who breaks up weighty matters of business by trifling with words]. Of which kind also, Plato in his *Protagoras*[13] bringeth in Prodicus in scorn, and maketh him make a speech that consisteth of distinctions from the beginning to the end. Generally such men, in all deliberations, find ease[14] to be of the negative side, and affect a credit to object and foretell[15] difficulties; for

2. There are men who, as far as wisdom and ability are concerned, do nothing. 3. Pretenders to wisdom. 4. Stereoscopic lenses to make objects in pictures look as if they were bodies with depth and bulk. 5. That. 6. That they are speaking about something which. 7. Wish nevertheless to make it seem to others that they know. 8. Manage. 9. Irrelevant or uselessly elaborate. 10. Subtle distinction. 11. Gloss over. 12. B. errs here; Quintilian, the Roman rhetorician, made a similar statement. 13. One of Plato's *Dialogues.* Prodicus and Protagoras taught philosophy in the fourth century B.C. 14. Find it easy. 15. Try to gain credit for objecting or foretelling.

when propositions are denied, there is an end of them; but if they be allowed, it requireth a new work; which false point of wisdom is the bane of business. To conclude, there is no decaying merchant or inward beggar[16] hath so many tricks to uphold the credit of their[17] wealth, as these empty persons have to maintain the credit of their sufficiency. Seeming wise men may make shift to get opinion,[18] but let no man choose them for employment; for certainly you were better take for business a man somewhat absurd than over-formal.[19]

XXVII. OF FRIENDSHIP

It had been hard for him[1] that spake it to have put more truth and untruth together in few words, than in that speech, "Whosoever is delighted in solitude is either a wild beast or a god." For it is most true that a natural and secret hatred and aversation towards society in any man hath somewhat of the savage beast, but it is most untrue that it should have any character at all of the divine nature, except it proceed, not out of a pleasure in solitude, but out of a love and desire to sequester a man's self for a higher conversation, such as is found to have been falsely and feignedly in some of the heathen; as Epimenides the Candian,[2] Numa[3] the Roman, Empedocles[4] the Sicilian, and Apollonius[5] of Tyana; and truly and really in divers of the ancient hermits and holy fathers of the church. But little do men perceive what solitude is, and how far it extendeth. For a crowd is not company; and faces are but a gallery of pictures; and talk but a tinkling cymbal, where there is no love. The Latin adage meeteth with it a little: *Magna civitas, magna solitudo* [A great city is a great soli-

16. A penniless man whose poverty is kept a secret known only to himself. 17. His. 18. To be well thought of. 19. It would be better for you to take for business a man who is somewhat ridiculous rather than one who is only a pretender to wisdom. 1. Aristotle, *Politics* I, i. 2. Poet of Crete (Candia), 6th century, reputed to have slept in a cave 57 years without waking. 3. Numa, 2nd king of Rome, claimed that a nymph taught him legislation in a cave. 4. Greek philosopher, 5th century B.C., said to have thrown himself into Mount Etna so that his disappearance might make him thought a god. 5. Philosopher and reputed worker of miracles, 1st century.

tude], because in a great town friends are scattered, so that
20 there is not that fellowship, for the most part, which is in less neighborhoods. But we may go further, and affirm most truly that it is a mere and miserable solitude to want true friends, without which the world is but a wilderness; and even in this sense also of solitude, whosoever in the frame of his nature and affections is unfit for friendship, he taketh it of the beast, and not from humanity.

A principal fruit of friendship is the ease and discharge of the fulness and swellings of the heart, which passions of all kinds do cause and induce. We know diseases of stoppings
30 and suffocations are the most dangerous in the body, and it is not much otherwise in the mind: you may take sarza [6] to open the liver, steel to open the spleen, flower of sulphur [7] for the lungs, castoreum [8] for the brain, but no receipt openeth the heart but a true friend to whom you may impart griefs, joys, fears, hopes, suspicions, counsels, and whatsoever lieth upon the heart to oppress it, in a kind of civil shrift or confession.

It is a strange thing to observe how high a rate great kings and monarchs do set upon this fruit of friendship whereof we
40 speak: so great, as they purchase it many times at the hazard of their own safety and greatness. For princes, in regard of the distance of their fortune from that of their subjects and servants, cannot gather this fruit, except (to make themselves capable thereof) they raise some persons to be as it were companions and almost equals to themselves, which many times sorteth to [9] inconvenience. The modern languages give unto such persons the name of favorites, or privadoes, as if it were matter of grace, or conversation. But the Roman name attaineth the true use and cause thereof, naming them *participes*
50 *curarum* [partners in cares], for it is that which tieth the knot. And we see plainly that this hath been done, not by weak and passionate princes only, but by the wisest and most politic that ever reigned, who have oftentimes joined to themselves some of their servants, whom both themselves have called friends, and allowed others likewise to call them in the same manner, using the word which is received between private men.

6. Sarsaparilla. 7. Purified sulphur. 8. An oily secretion of beavers. 9. Becomes.

L. Sylla,[10] when he commanded Rome, raised Pompey[11] (after surnamed the Great) to that height, that Pompey vaunted himself for Sylla's over-match. For when he had carried the consulship for a friend of his, against the pursuit of Sylla, and that Sylla did a little resent thereat, and began to speak great, Pompey turned upon him again, and in effect bade him be quiet; "for that more men adored the sun rising than the sun setting." With Julius Cæsar, Decimus Brutus[12] had obtained that interest, as he set him down in his testament for heir in remainder after his nephew. And this was the man that had power with him to draw him forth to his death. For when Cæsar would have discharged the senate, in regard of some ill presages, and specially a dream of Calpurnia, this man lifted him gently by the arm out of his chair, telling him he hoped he would not dismiss the senate till his wife had dreamt a better dream. And it seemeth his favor was so great, as Antonius, in a letter which is recited *verbatim* in one of Cicero's Philippics, calleth him "venefica," *witch,* as if he had enchanted Cæsar. Augustus[13] raised Agrippa[12] (though of mean birth) to that height, as when he consulted with Mæcenas[12] about the marriage of his daughter Julia, Mæcenas took the liberty to tell him, "that he must either marry his daughter to Agrippa, or take away his life: there was no third way, he had made him so great." With Tiberius Cæsar,[13] Sejanus[12] had ascended to that height, as they two were termed and reckoned as a pair of friends. Tiberius in a letter to him saith, *Hæc pro amicitia nostra non occultavi* [Because of our friendship, I have not concealed these things]; and the whole senate dedicated an altar to Friendship, as to a goddess, in respect of the great dearness of friendship between them two. The like or more was between Septimius Severus[13] and Plautianus.[12] For he forced his eldest son to marry the daughter of Plautianus, and would often maintain Plautianus in doing affronts to his son, and did write also in a letter to the senate, by these words: "I love the man so well, as I wish he may over-live me." Now if these princes had been as a Trajan[13] or a Marcus Aurelius,[13] a man might have thought that this had proceeded of an abundant goodness of nature, but being men so wise, of such strength and severity of mind, and so extreme lovers of themselves as all these were, it proveth

10. Sulla, d. 78 B.C., Roman dictator. 11. Roman general, d. 48 B.C. 12. Roman statesman. 13. Roman emperor.

most plainly that they found their own felicity (though as great as ever happened to mortal men) but as an half piece, ex-
100 cept they mought[14] have a friend to make it entire; and yet, which is more, they were princes that had wives, sons, nephews; and yet all these could not supply the comfort of friendship.

It is not to be forgotten what Comineus[15] observeth of his first master, Duke Charles the Hardy;[16] namely, that he would communicate his secrets with none, and least of all, those secrets which troubled him most. Whereupon he goeth on and saith that towards his latter time "that closeness did impair and a little perish his understanding." Surely Comin-
110 eus mought have made the same judgment also, if it had pleased him, of his second master, Lewis the Eleventh,[17] whose closeness was indeed his tormentor. The parable[18] of Pythagoras[19] is dark, but true; *Cor ne edito*: "Eat not the heart." Certainly, if a man would give it a hard phrase, those that want friends to open themselves unto are cannibals of their own hearts. But one thing is most admirable (wherewith I will conclude this first fruit of friendship), which is, that this communicating of a man's self to his friend works two contrary effects, for it redoubleth joys and cutteth griefs in
120 halves. For there is no man that imparteth his joys to his friend, but he joyeth the more; and no man that imparteth his griefs to his friend, but he grieveth the less. So that it is in truth of operation upon a man's mind, of like virtue[20] as the alchemists use to attribute to their stone[21] for man's body, that it worketh all contrary effects, but still[22] to the good and benefit of nature. But yet without praying in aid of[23] alchemists, there is a manifest image of this in the ordinary course of nature. For in bodies,[24] union strengtheneth and cherisheth any natural action, and on the other side weaken-
130 eth and dulleth any violent impression, and even so it is of minds.

The second fruit of friendship is healthful and sovereign[25] for the understanding, as the first is for the affections. For

14. Might. 15. Philippe de Comines, French historian, d. 1509. 16. Charles the Bold, Duke of Burgundy, d. 1477. 17. King of France, d. 1483. 18. Metaphor. 19. Greek philosopher, 6th century B.C. 20. Power. 21. The "philosopher's stone," a substance which would transmute baser metals into gold or cure bodily diseases. Alchemists were the scientists who sought it. 22. Always. 23. Making a case for. 24. All material bodies. 25. Supreme in power.

friendship maketh indeed a fair day in the affections, from storm and tempests; but it maketh daylight in the understanding, out of darkness and confusion of thoughts. Neither is this to be understood only of faithful counsel, which a man receiveth from his friend; but before you come to that, certain it is that whosoever hath his mind fraught with many thoughts, his wits and understanding do clarify and break up, 140 in the communicating and discoursing with another; he tosseth his thoughts more easily; he marshalleth them more orderly; he seeth how they look when they are turned into words: finally, he waxeth wiser than himself; and that more by an hour's discourse than by a day's meditation. It was well said by Themistocles [26] to the king of Persia, "that speech was like cloth of Arras,[27] opened and put abroad; whereby the imagery doth appear in figure; whereas in thoughts they lie but as in packs." Neither is this second fruit of friendship, in opening the understanding, restrained only to such friends 150 as are able to give a man counsel (they indeed are best), but even without that, a man learneth of himself and bringeth his own thoughts to light and whetteth his wits as against a stone, which itself cuts not. In a word, a man were better relate himself to a statua or picture, than to suffer his thoughts to pass in smother.

Add now, to make this second fruit of friendship complete, that other point which lieth more open and falleth within vulgar observation, which is faithful counsel from a friend. Heraclitus [28] saith well in one of his enigmas, "Dry light is 160 ever the best." And certain it is, that the light that a man receiveth by counsel from another is drier and purer than that which cometh from his own understanding and judgment, which is ever infused and drenched in his affections and customs. So as there is as much difference between the counsel that a friend giveth and that a man giveth himself, as there is between the counsel of a friend and of a flatterer. For there is no such flatterer as is a man's self, and there is no such remedy against flattery of a man's self as the liberty of a friend. Counsel is of two sorts: the one concerning manners,[29] the 170

26. Athenian general and statesman, d. 460 B.C. 27. French city noted for tapestry. 28. Greek philosopher, d. 475 B.C. He taught that the dry light of reason (i.e., a mind not "wet" or intoxicated) is always better as a source and standard of truth than knowledge influenced by appetites, feelings, senses or customs. 29. Morals.

other concerning business. For the first, the best preservative to keep the mind in health is the faithful admonition of a friend. The calling of a man's self to a strict account is a medicine sometime too piercing and corrosive. Reading good books of morality is a little flat and dead. Observing our faults in others is sometimes improper for our case. But the best receipt (best, I say, to work, and best to take) is the admonition of a friend. It is a strange thing to behold what gross errors and extreme absurdities many (especially of the greater sort) do
180 commit for want of a friend to tell them of them, to the great damage both of their fame and fortune, for, as St. James saith, they are as men "that look sometimes into a glass, and presently forget their own shape and favor." As for business, a man may think, if he will, that two eyes see no more than one; or that a gamester seeth always more than a looker-on; or that a man in anger is as wise as he that hath said over the four and twenty letters;[30] or that a musket may be shot off as well upon the arm as upon a rest; and such other fond and high imaginations, to think himself all in all. But when all is done,
190 the help of good counsel is that which setteth business straight. And if any man think that he will take counsel, but it shall be by pieces, asking counsel in one business of one man, and in another business of another man, it is well (that is to say, better perhaps than if he asked none at all). But he runneth two dangers: one, that he shall not be faithfully counseled, for it is a rare thing, except it be from a perfect and entire friend, to have counsel given, but such as shall be bowed and crooked to some ends which he hath that giveth it. The other, that he shall have counsel given, hurtful and unsafe (though
200 with good meaning), and mixed partly of mischief and partly of remedy; even as if you would call a physician that is thought good for the cure of the disease you complain of, but is unacquainted with your body, and therefore may put you in way for a present cure, but overthroweth your health in some other kind; and so cure the disease and kill the patient. But a friend that is wholly acquainted with a man's estate will beware, by furthering any present business, how he dasheth upon other inconvenience. And therefore rest not upon scat-

30. I and J were regarded as the same letter; likewise U and V; hence, 24 letters of the alphabet, recited to control anger, just as today we "count to ten" while tempers cool.

tered counsels; they will rather distract and mislead, than settle and direct. 210

After these two noble fruits of friendship (peace in the affections, and support of the judgment), followeth the last fruit, which is like the pomegranate, full of many kernels. I mean aid and bearing a part in all actions and occasions. Here the best way to represent to life the manifold use of friendship is to cast[31] and see how many things there are which a man cannot do himself, and then it will appear that it was a sparing speech of the ancients, to say, "that a friend is another himself," for that a friend is far more than himself. Men have their time, and die many times in desire of some 220 things which they principally take to heart: the bestowing of a child, the finishing of a work, or the like. If a man have a true friend, he may rest almost secure that the care of those things will continue after him. So that a man hath, as it were, two lives in his desires. A man hath a body, and that body is confined to a place; but where friendship is, all offices of life are as it were granted to him and his deputy, for he may exercise them by his friend. How many things are there which a man cannot, with any face or comeliness, say or do himself? A man can scarce allege his own merits with modesty, much 230 less extol them; a man cannot sometimes brook to supplicate or beg; and a number of the like. But all these things are graceful in a friend's mouth, which are blushing in a man's own. So again, a man's person hath many proper relations which he cannot put off. A man cannot speak to his son but as a father; to his wife but as a husband; to his enemy but upon terms: whereas a friend may speak as the case requires, and not as it sorteth with[32] the person. But to enumerate these things were endless; I have given the rule: Where a man cannot fitly play his own part, if he have not a friend, he may quit the stage. 240

31. Stop and consider. | 32. Suits.

XXVIII. OF EXPENSE

Riches are for spending; and spending, for honor and good actions. Therefore extraordinary expense must be limited by the worth of the occasion, for voluntary undoing may be as well for a man's country as for the kingdom of heaven. But ordinary expense ought to be limited by a man's estate, and governed with such regard, as it be within his compass,[1] and not subject to deceit and abuse of servants, and ordered to the best show, that the bills may be less than the estimation abroad. Certainly, if a man will keep but of even hand,[2] his
10 ordinary expenses ought to be but to the half of his receipts; and if he think to wax rich, but to the third part. It is no baseness for the greatest to descend and look into their own estate. Some forbear it, not upon negligence alone, but doubting [3] to bring themselves into melancholy, in respect they shall find it broken. But wounds cannot be cured without searching. He that cannot look into his own estate at all, had need both choose well those whom he employeth, and change them often; for new are more timorous and less subtle. He that can look into his estate but seldom, it behooveth him to turn all
20 to certainties.[4] A man hath need, if he be plentiful in some kind of expense, to be as saving again in some other. As if he be plentiful in diet, to be saving in apparel; if he be plentiful in the hall, to be saving in the stable; and the like. For he that is plentiful in expenses of all kinds will hardly be preserved from decay. In clearing of a man's estate, he may as well hurt himself in being too sudden, as in letting it run on too long. For hasty selling is commonly as disadvantageable as interest. Besides, he that clears at once will relapse, for finding himself out of straits, he will revert to his customs; but he that clear-
30 eth by degrees induceth a habit of frugality, and gaineth as well upon his mind as upon his estate. Certainly who hath a state [5] to repair may not despise small things, and commonly it is less dishonorable to abridge petty charges than to stoop to petty gettings. A man ought warily to begin charges which once begun will continue, but in matters that return not he may be more magnificent.

1. And regulated with regard to what he can afford. 2. If a man wishes to maintain himself on his present level of wealth, without fluctuations. 3. Fearing. 4. Fixed income and expenditures. 5. An estate.

XXX. OF REGIMENT OF HEALTH

There is a wisdom in this beyond the rules of physic: a man's own observation, what he finds good of,[1] and what he finds hurt of, is the best physic to preserve health. But it is a safer conclusion to say, "This agreeth not well with me, therefore I will not continue it," than this, "I find no offence of [2] this; therefore I may use it"; for strength of nature in youth passeth over many excesses which are owing a man [3] till his age. Discern of the coming on of years, and think not to do the same things still; for age will not be defied. Beware of sudden change in any great point of diet, and if necessity 10 enforce it, fit the rest to it; for it is a secret both in nature and state, that it is safer to change many things than one. Examine thy customs of diet, sleep, exercise, apparel and the like, and try in anything thou shalt judge hurtful, to discontinue it by little and little; but so as [4] if thou dost find any inconvenience by the change, thou come back to it again; for it is hard to distinguish that which is generally held good and wholesome from that which is good particularly and fit for thine own body. To be free-minded and cheerfully disposed at hours of meat [5] and of sleep and of exercise is one of the best precepts 20 of long lasting. As for the passions and studies of the mind, avoid envy, anxious fears, anger fretting inwards, subtle and knotty inquisitions, joys and exhilarations in excess, sadness not communicated. Entertain hopes, mirth rather than joy, variety of delights rather than surfeit of them; wonder and admiration, and therefore novelties; studies that fill the mind with splendid and illustrious objects, as histories, fables, and contemplations of nature. If you fly physic in health altogether, it will be too strange for your body when you shall need it; if you make it too familiar, it will work no extraordi- 30 nary effect when sickness cometh. I commend rather some diet for certain seasons than frequent use of physic, except it be grown into a custom; for those diets alter the body more, and trouble it less. Despise no new accident in your body, but ask opinion of it.[6] In sickness, respect [7] health principally; and in

1. From. 2. Harm from. 3. Which a man is not bound to pay for. 4. But conduct yourself in such a manner that. 5. Meals. 6. Ask for medical advice about it. 7. Pay attention to.

health, action: for those that put their bodies to endure in health may, in most sicknesses which are not very sharp, be cured only with diet and tendering.[8] Celsus [9] could never have spoken it as a physician, had he not been a wise man withal,
40 when he giveth it for one of the great precepts of health and lasting, that a man do vary and interchange contraries, but with an inclination to the more benign extreme: use fasting and full eating, but rather full eating; watching [10] and sleep, but rather sleep; sitting and exercise, but rather exercise; and the like. So shall nature be cherished and yet taught masteries.[11] Physicians are some of them so pleasing and conformable to the humor [12] of the patient, as [13] they press not the true cure of the disease; and some other are so regular in proceeding according to art for the disease as [13] they respect not
50 sufficiently the condition of the patient. Take one of a middle temper,[14] or if it may not be found in one man, combine two of either sort; and forget not to call as well the best acquainted with your body, as the best reputed of for his faculty.[15]

XXXI. OF SUSPICION

Suspicions amongst thoughts are like bats amongst birds: they ever fly by twilight. Certainly they are to be repressed or at least well guarded,[1] for they cloud the mind; they leese [2] friends; and they check [3] with business, whereby business cannot go on currently [4] and constantly. They dispose kings to tyranny, husbands to jealousy, wise men to irresolution and melancholy. They are defects, not in the heart [5] but in the brain; for they take place in the stoutest [6] natures, as in the example of Henry the Seventh of England. There was not a
10 more suspicious man nor a more stout. And in such a composition [7] they do small hurt, for commonly they are not admitted

8. Careful nursing. B. had a feeble constitution which often required medicine or careful dieting. 9. Roman writer on medicine. 10. Staying awake. 11. Mastery over disease. 12. Caprices. 13. That. 14. A physician whose nature is midway between these two types. 15. Ability. 1. Controlled. 2. Lose. 3. Interfere. 4. Uninterruptedly. 5. Regarded as the seat of courage (from Latin *cor,* heart). 6. Most resolute. 7. Nature.

but with examination whether they be likely or no;[8] but in fearful natures they gain ground too fast. There is nothing makes a man suspect much, more than to know little; and therefore men should remedy suspicion by procuring to know more, and not to keep their suspicions in smother.[9] What would men have? Do they think those they employ and deal with are saints? Do they not think they will have their own ends, and be truer to themselves than to them? Therefore there is no better way to moderate suspicions, than to account 20 upon such suspicions as true and yet to bridle them as false.[10] For so far a man ought to make use of suspicions, as to provide, as if that should be true that he suspects, yet it may do him no hurt. Suspicions that the mind of itself gathers are but buzzes, but suspicions that are artificially nourished and put into men's heads by the tales and whisperings of others have stings. Certainly the best mean to clear the way in this same wood of suspicions is frankly to communicate them with the party that he suspects, for thereby he shall be sure to know more of the truth of them than he did before, and withal shall 30 make that party more circumspect not to give further cause of suspicion. But this would not be done to men of base natures, for they, if they find themselves once suspected, will never be true. The Italian says, *Sospetto licentia fede* [Suspicion permits faith to depart], as if suspicion did give a passport to faith; but it ought rather to kindle it to discharge itself.

XXXII. OF DISCOURSE

Some in their discourse desire rather commendation of wit,[1] in being able to hold all arguments, than of judgment, in discerning what is true, as if it were a praise to know what might be said, and not what should be thought. Some have certain common places and themes wherein they are good, and want variety, which kind of poverty is for the most part tedious, and when it is once perceived, ridiculous. The honorablest part of

8. Commonly the minds of such men do not admit suspicions without testing their likelihood. 9. Suppressed. 10. To prepare for them as if they were true, but to hold back from believing them, as if they were false. 1. For cleverness.

talk is to give the occasion,[2] and again to moderate[3] and pass to somewhat else, for then a man leads the dance. It is good, in discourse and speech of conversation, to vary and intermingle speech of the present occasion with arguments, tales with reasons, asking of questions with telling of opinions, and jest with earnest; for it is a dull thing to tire, and, as we say now, to jade[4] any thing too far. As for jest, there be certain things which ought to be privileged from it; namely, religion, matters of state, great persons, any man's present business of importance, and any case that deserveth pity. Yet there be some that think their wits have been asleep, except they dart out somewhat that is piquant and to the quick.[5] That is a vein which would be[6] bridled; *Parce, puer, stimulis, et fortius utere loris* [Be sparing with the whip, boy, and grasp the reins more firmly]. And generally, men ought to find the difference between saltness[7] and bitterness. Certainly, he that hath a satirical vein, as he maketh others afraid of his wit, so he had need be afraid of others' memory. He that questioneth much shall learn much and content[8] much, but especially if he apply his questions to the skill of the persons whom he asketh; for he shall give them occasion to please themselves in speaking, and himself shall continually gather knowledge. But let his questions not be troublesome, for that is fit for a poser.[9] And let him be sure to leave other men their turns to speak. Nay, if there be any that would reign and take up all the time, let him find means to take them off and to bring others on, as musicians use to do with those that dance too long galliards.[10] If you dissemble sometimes your knowledge of that you are thought to know, you shall be thought another time to know that you know not. Speech of[11] a man's self ought to be seldom and well chosen. I knew one was wont to say in scorn, "He must needs be a wise man, he speaks so much of himself." And there is but one case wherein a man may commend himself with good grace, and that is in commending virtue in another, especially if it be such a virtue whereunto himself pretendeth. Speech of touch towards others[12] should be sparingly used, for discourse ought to be as a field, without coming home to any man. I knew two noble-

2. Suggest the topic of conversation. 3. Regulate. 4. Ride. 5. In the nature of repartee. 6. Needs to be. 7. Piquant humor. 8. Please. 9. Examiner. 10. Lively French dances. 11. About. 12. Remarks that hit at individuals.

men, of the west part of England, whereof the one was given to scoff, but kept ever royal cheer in his house; the other would ask of those that had been at the other's table, "Tell truly, was there never a flout[13] or dry blow[14] given?" To which the guest would answer, "Such and such a thing passed." The lord would say, "I thought he would mar a good dinner." Discretion of speech is more than eloquence; and to speak agreeably[15] to him with whom we deal is more than to speak in good words or in good order. A good continued speech, without a good speech of interlocution, shows slowness; and a good reply or second speech, without a good settled speech, showeth shallowness and weakness. As we see in beasts, that those that are weakest in the course are yet nimblest in the turn, as it is betwixt the greyhound and the hare. To use too many circumstances[16] ere one come to the matter is wearisome; to use none at all is blunt.

XXXIII. OF PLANTATIONS

Plantations[1] are amongst ancient, primitive, and heroical works. When the world was young it begat more children, but now it is old, it begets fewer;[2] for I may justly account new plantations to be the children of former kingdoms. I like a plantation in a pure soil, that is, where people are not displanted to the end to plant in others; for else it is rather an extirpation than a plantation. Planting of countries is like planting of woods; for you must make account to lose almost twenty years' profit, and expect your recompense in the end; for the principal thing that hath been the destruction of most plantations, hath been the base and hasty drawing of profit in the first years. It is true, speedy profit is not to be neglected, as far as it may stand[3] with the good of the plantation, but no farther.

It is a shameful and unblessed thing to take the scum of

13. Jibe. 14. Sarcastic remark. 15. In a way suited. 16. Preliminary details. 1. Colonies. 2. There was a widespread belief in Bacon's day that nature was decaying and that the universe, including mankind, was declining into weakness and impotence. 3. Be consistent.

people and wicked condemned men, to be the people with whom you plant; and not only so, but it spoileth the plantation; for they will ever live like rogues, and not fall to work, but be lazy, and do mischief, and spend victuals, and be
20 quickly weary, and then certify [4] over to their country to the discredit of the plantation. The people wherewith you plant ought to be gardeners, ploughmen, laborers, smiths, carpenters, joiners, fishermen, fowlers, with some few apothecaries, surgeons, cooks, and bakers. In a country of plantation, first look about what kind of victual the country yields of itself to hand, as chestnuts, walnuts, pine-apples, olives, dates, plums, cherries, wild honey, and the like, and make use of them. Then consider what victual or esculent things there are, which grow speedily, and within the year, as parsnips, carrots, tur-
30 nips, onions, radish, artichokes of Jerusalem, maize, and the like. For wheat, barley, and oats, they ask too much labor; but with peas and beans you may begin, both because they ask less labor, and because they serve for meat as well as for bread; and of rice likewise cometh a great increase, and it is a kind of meat. Above all, there ought to be brought store of biscuit, oatmeal, flour, meal, and the like, in the beginning, till bread may be had. For beasts or birds, take chiefly such as are least subject to diseases and multiply fastest, as swine, goats, cocks, hens, turkeys, geese, house-doves, and the like. The victual in
40 plantations ought to be expended almost as in a besieged town, that is, with certain allowance. And let the main part of the ground employed to [5] gardens or corn be to [6] a common stock, and to be laid in, and stored up, and then delivered out in proportion; besides some spots of ground that any particular person will manure for his own private.[7] Consider likewise what commodities the soil where the plantation is doth naturally yield, that they may some way help to defray the charge of the plantation, so [8] it be not, as was said, to the untimely prejudice of the main business, as it hath fared with tobacco in Vir-
50 ginia. Wood commonly aboundeth but too much, and therefore timber is fit to be one.[9] If there be iron ore and streams whereupon to set the mills, iron is a brave [10] commodity where wood aboundeth. Making a bay salt,[11] if the climate be proper for it, would be put in experience.[12] Growing silk,

4. Report. 5. In. 6. For. 7. Private use. 8. So arranging matters that. 9. One of the commodities. 10. Excellent. 11. Making salt by evaporating sea-water. 12. Should be tried.

likewise, if any be, is a likely commodity. Pitch and tar, where store of firs and pines are, will not fail. So drugs and sweet woods, where they are, cannot but yield great profit. Soap ashes likewise, and other things that may be thought of. But moil [13] not too much under ground, for the hope of mines is very uncertain, and useth to make the planters lazy in other things. For government, let it be in the hands of one, assisted with some counsel; and let them have commission to exercise martial laws, with some limitation. And, above all, let men make that profit of being in the wilderness, as [14] they have God always and his service before their eyes. Let not the government of the plantation depend upon too many counsellors and undertakers [15] in the country that planteth, but upon a temperate number; and let those be rather noblemen and gentlemen, than merchants, for they look ever to the present gain. Let there be freedoms from custom,[16] till the plantation be of strength, and not only freedom from custom, but freedom to carry their commodities where they may make their best of them, except there be some special cause of caution. Cram not in people by sending too fast, company after company, but rather hearken [17] how they waste, and send supplies proportionably; but so as the number may live well in the plantation, and not by surcharge be in penury. It hath been a great endangering to the health of some plantations, that they have built along the sea and rivers, in marish [18] and unwholesome grounds; therefore, though you begin there, to avoid carriage and other like discommodities, yet build still rather upwards from the stream, than along it. It concerneth likewise the health of the plantation that they have good store of salt with them, that they may use it in their victuals when it shall be necessary.

If you plant where savages are, do not only entertain them with trifles and gingles, but use them justly and graciously, with sufficient guard, nevertheless; and do not win their favor by helping them to invade their enemies, but for their defense, it is not amiss; and send oft of them to the country that plants, that they may see a better condition than their own, and commend it when they return.

When the plantation grows to strength, then it is time to plant with women as well as with men, that the plantation

13. Toil. 14. That. 15. Managers. 16. Export and import duties. 17. Observe. 18. Marshy.

may spread into generations, and not be ever pieced from without. It is the sinfullest thing in the world to forsake or destitute[19] a plantation once in forwardness; for, besides the dishonor, it is the guiltiness of blood of many commiserable[20] persons.

XXXIV. OF RICHES

I cannot call riches better than the baggage of virtue. The Roman word is better, *impedimenta*.[1] For as the baggage is to an army, so is riches to virtue. It cannot be spared nor left behind, but it hindereth the march; yea, and the care of it sometimes loseth or disturbeth the victory. Of great riches there is no real use, except it be in the distribution; the rest is but conceit.[2] So saith Solomon, "Where much is, there are many to consume it; and what hath the owner but the sight of it with his eyes?" The personal fruition in any
10 man cannot reach to feel great riches:[3] there is a custody of them, or a power of dole and donative of them, or a fame of them, but no solid use to the owner. Do you not see what feigned prices are set upon little stones and rarities, and what works of ostentation are undertaken, because[4] there might seem to be some us of great riches? But then you will say, they may be of use to buy men out of dangers or troubles. As Solomon saith, "Riches are as a stronghold in the imagination of the rich man." But this is excellently expressed, that it is in imagination and not always in fact. For certainly great riches
20 have sold more men than they have bought out. Seek not proud riches, but such as thou mayest get justly, use soberly, distribute cheerfully, and leave contentedly. Yet have no abstract[5] nor friarly contempt of them. But distinguish, as Cicero saith well of Rabirius Posthumus, *In studio rei amplificandæ apparebat, non avaritiæ prædam, sed instrumentum bonitati quæri* [In his zeal for increasing his wealth, it was

19. Leave destitute. 20. Worthy of compassion. 1. Literally: the hindering things, impediments; hence, the baggage of an army. 2. Imagination. 3. A man's capacity for personal enjoyment is too limited for him to experience everything which great riches may bring. 4. In order that. 5. Withdrawn from life; impractical.

apparent that he sought not a prey for avarice but an instrument for good]. Harken also to Solomon, and beware of hasty gathering of riches; *Qui festinat ad divitias, non erit insons* [He that maketh haste to be rich shall not be innocent]. The 30 poets feign that when Plutus (which is Riches) is sent from Jupiter, he limps and goes slowly, but when he is sent from Pluto, he runs and is swift of foot; meaning that riches gotten by good means and just labor pace slowly, but when they come by the death of others (as by the course of inheritance, testaments, and the like), they come tumbling upon a man. But it mought [6] be applied likewise to Pluto, taking him for the devil: for when riches come from the devil (as by fraud and oppression and unjust means), they come upon speed. The ways to enrich are many, and most of them foul. Parsi- 40 mony is one of the best, and yet is not innocent, for it withholdeth men from works of liberality and charity. The improvement of the ground is the most natural obtaining of riches, for it is our great mother's blessing, the earth's, but it is slow. And yet where men of great wealth do stoop to husbandry, it multiplieth riches exceedingly. I knew a nobleman in England, that had the greatest audits [7] of any man in my time; a great grazier, a great sheepmaster, a great timber man, a great collier, a great corn-master, a great lead-man, and so of iron, and a number of the like points of husbandry; so as 50 the earth seemed a sea to him, in respect of the perpetual importation. It was truly observed by one, that himself came very hardly [8] to a little riches, and very easily to great riches. For when a man's stock is come to that, that he can expect [9] the prime of markets, and overcome those bargains which for their greatness are few men's money,[10] and be partner in the industries of younger men, he cannot but increase mainly.[11] The gains of ordinary trades and vocations are honest, and furthered by two things chiefly, by diligence and by a good name for good and fair dealing. But the gains of bargains 60 are of a more doubtful nature, when men shall wait upon others' necessity, broke by servants and instruments [12] to draw them on, put off others cunningly that would be better chap-

6. Might. 7. Income-roll. 8. He himself arrived with great difficulty. 9. Wait for. 10. And be capable of taking advantage of those bargains which are so expensive that few men have enough money for them. 11. Greatly. 12. Do business by using servants and contrivances.

men,[13] and the like practices, which are crafty and naught.[14] As for the chopping of[15] bargains, when a man buys not to hold but to sell over again, that commonly grindeth double, both upon the seller and upon the buyer.[16] Sharings do greatly enrich, if the hands be well chosen that are trusted. Usury is the certainest means of gain, though one of the worst, as that
70 whereby a man doth eat his bread *in sudore vultus alieni* [in the sweat of another man's face],[17] and besides, doth plow upon Sundays. But yet certain though it be, it hath flaws, for that the scriveners[18] and brokers do value unsound men[19] to serve their own turn. The fortune in being the first in an invention or in a privilege doth cause sometimes a wonderful overgrowth in riches, as it was with the first sugar man in the Canaries. Therefore if a man can play the true logician, to have as well judgment as invention, he may do great matters especially if the times be fit. He that resteth
80 upon gains certain shall hardly grow to great riches, and he that puts all upon adventures[20] doth oftentimes break and come to poverty: it is good therefore to guard adventures with certainties, that may uphold losses. Monopolies and coemption[21] of wares for re-sale, where they are not restrained, are great means to enrich, especially if the party have intelligence what things are like to come into request, and so store himself beforehand. Riches gotten by service, though it be of the best rise,[22] yet when they are gotten by flattery, feeding humors,[23] and other servile conditions, they may be placed
90 amongst the worst. As for fishing for testaments and executorships (as Tacitus saith of Seneca, *testamenta et orbos tamquam indagine capi* [he seized wills and wardships as with a net]), it is yet worse, by how much men submit themselves to meaner persons than in service. Believe not much them that seem to despise riches, for they despise them that despair of them; and none worse when they come to them.[24] Be not

13. Buyers. 14. Bad. 15. Dealing in. "Chop" means exchange or barter. 16. Oppresses doubly, bearing hard on both the original seller and the final buyer. 17. Cf. *Genesis,* iii, 19. 18. Moneylenders. 19. Misrepresent men who are financially unsound as if they were good risks. 20. Speculations. 21. Buying up commodities to control the market; a corner. 22. Though the getting of the wealth is from the best source. The Latin text reads: "though it have a certain dignity." 23. Catering to whims. 24. For those men who are discouraged about getting riches despise riches; and no men despise riches more than those who have attained them.

penny-wise; riches have wings, and sometimes they fly away of themselves, sometimes they must be set flying to bring in more. Men leave their riches either to their kindred or to the public, and moderate portions prosper best in both. A great state left to an heir is as a lure to all the birds of prey round about to seize on him, if he be not the better stablished in years and judgment. Likewise glorious gifts and foundations are like "sacrifices without salt," and but the painted sepulchers of alms, which soon will putrefy and corrupt inwardly. Therefore measure not thine advancements [25] by quantity, but frame them by measure: [26] and defer not charities till death for, certainly, if a man weigh it rightly, he that doth so is rather liberal of another man's than of his own. 100

XXXVI. OF AMBITION

Ambition is like choler, which is an humor [1] that maketh men active, earnest, full of alacrity, and stirring, if it be not stopped, but if it be stopped, and cannot have his way, it becometh adust,[2] and thereby malign and venomous. So ambitious men, if they find the way open for their rising, and still get forward, they are rather busy than dangerous; but if they be checked in their desires, they become secretly discontent and look upon men and matters with an evil eye, and are best pleased when things go backward, which is the worst property [3] in a servant of a prince or state. Therefore it is good for princes, if they use ambitious men, to handle it so as they be still progressive and not retrograde,[4] which because it cannot be without inconvenience, it is good not to use such natures at all. For if they rise not with their service, they will take order [5] to make their service fall with them. But since we have said it were good not to use men of ambitious natures except it be upon necessity, it is fit we speak in what cases they are of necessity. Good commanders in the wars must be taken be they never so ambitious, for the use of their service 10

25. Gifts. 26. Regulate them according to their suitability and appropriateness. 1. A fluid in the human body. 2. Bilious and fretful. 3. The worst possible characteristic. 4. So that they will always be making progress and not falling back. 5. Order matters.

20 dispenseth with the rest; and to take a soldier without ambition is to pull off his spurs. There is also great use of ambitious men in being screens to princes in matters of danger and envy, for no man will take that part, except he be like a seeled dove,[6] that mounts and mounts because he cannot see about him. There is use also of ambitious men in pulling down the greatness of any subject that overtops; as Tiberius[7] used Macro[8] in the pulling down of Sejanus.[9] Since therefore they must be used in such cases, there resteth to speak how they are to be bridled that they may be less dangerous. There is less
30 danger of them if they be of mean birth, than if they be noble; and if they be rather harsh of nature, than gracious and popular; and if they be rather new raised, than grown cunning[10] and fortified in their greatness. It is counted by some a weakness in princes to have favorites, but it is of all others the best remedy against ambitious great ones. For when the way of pleasuring and displeasuring lieth by the favorite, it is impossible any other should be over-great. Another means to curb them is to balance them by others as proud as they. But then there must be some middle counsellors to keep
40 things steady, for without that ballast the ship will roll too much. At the least, a prince may animate and inure[11] some meaner persons, to be as it were scourges to ambitious men. As for the having of them obnoxious[12] to ruin, if they be of fearful natures, it may do well, but if they be stout[13] and daring, it may precipitate their designs and prove dangerous. As for the pulling of them down, if the affairs require it, and that it may not be done with safety suddenly, the only way is the interchange continually of favors and disgraces, whereby they may not know what to expect, and be as it were in a
50 wood. Of ambitions, it is less harmful, the ambition to prevail in great things, than that other, to appear in every thing, for that breeds confusion, and mars business. But yet it is less danger to have an ambitious man stirring in business, than great in dependences.[14] He that seeketh to be eminent amongst able men hath a great task, but that is ever good for the public. But he that plots to be the only figure amongst ciphers is the decay of a whole age. Honor hath three things

6. A dove whose eyelids have been pulled down with a thread drawn through them. 7. Roman emperor. 8. Roman general and courtier. 9. Roman courtier. 10. Ingenious through experience. 11. Habituate. 12. Liable. 13. Bold. 14. Retainers.

in it: the vantage ground to do good, the approach to kings and principal persons, and the raising of a man's own fortunes. He that hath the best of these intentions, when he aspireth, is an honest man; and that prince that can discern of these intentions in another that aspireth is a wise prince. Generally let princes and states choose such ministers as are more sensible of duty than of rising, and such as love business rather upon conscience than upon bravery,[15] and let them discern a busy nature from a willing mind. 60

XXXVII. OF MASQUES[1] AND TRIUMPHS[2]

These things are but toys, to come amongst such serious observations. But yet, since princes will have such things, it is better they should be graced with elegancy than daubed with cost. Dancing to song is a thing of great state and pleasure. I understand it, that the song be in quire, placed aloft, and accompanied with some broken music,[3] and the ditty fitted to the device.[4] Acting in song, especially in dialogues, hath an extreme good grace; I say acting, not dancing (for that is a mean and vulgar thing); and the voices of the dialogue would[5] be strong and manly (a base and a tenor; no treble[6]); 10 and the ditty high and tragical,[7] not nice or dainty. Several quires, placed one over against another, and taking the voice by catches,[8] anthem-wise, give great pleasure. Turning dances into figure[9] is a childish curiosity. And generally let it be noted, that those things which I here set down are such as do naturally take the sense,[10] and not respect[11] petty wonderments. It is true, the alterations of scenes, so it be quietly and without noise, are things of great beauty and pleasure, for they

15. Out of a sense of duty rather than a desire for display. 1. Elaborate dramatic performances for special celebrations, consisting chiefly of dancing and pantomime; the actors wore masks. 2. Pageants. 3. Music divided into parts arranged for different instruments. 4. Words appropriate to the general scheme of the dancing and action. 5. Should. 6. That is, no boy actors, perhaps. 7. Lofty and serious. 8. Having the different voices make contrapuntal entrances; cf. the entrances of voices in turn in a round like "Three Blind Mice." 9. Having the dancers arrange themselves to spell out names of persons present, and the like. 10. Appeal to the senses. 11. Concern.

feed and relieve the eye before it be full of the same object. Let
20 the scenes abound with light, specially colored and varied, and let the masquers or any other, that are to come down from the scene have some motions upon the scene itself before their coming down, for it draws the eye strangely and makes it with great pleasure to desire to see that it cannot perfectly discern. Let the songs be loud and cheerful and not chirpings or pulings. Let the music likewise be sharp and loud and well placed. The colors that show best by candle-light are white, carnation, and a kind of sea-water-green; and oes[12] or spangs,[13] as they are of no great cost, so they are of most glory.
30 As for rich embroidery, it is lost and not discerned. Let the suits of the masquers be graceful and such as become the person when the vizors are off, not after examples of known attires: Turks, soldiers, mariners, and the like. Let anti-masques[14] not be long; they have been commonly of fools, satyrs, baboons, wild-men, antics, beasts, sprites, witches, Ethiops, pigmies, turquets,[15] nymphs, rustics, Cupids, statuas moving, and the like. As for angels, it is not comical enough to put them in anti-masques; and anything that is hideous, as devils, giants, is on the other side[16] as unfit. But chiefly, let
40 the music of them be recreative and with some strange changes. Some sweet odors suddenly coming forth without any drops falling are, in such a company as there is steam and heat, things of great pleasure and refreshment. Double masques, one of men, another of ladies, addeth state and variety. But all is nothing except the room be kept clear and neat.

For justs[17] and tourneys[18] and barriers,[19] the glories of them are chiefly in the chariots wherein the challengers make their entry, especially if they be drawn with strange beasts, as
50 lions, bears, camels, and the like, or in the devices of their entrance; or in the bravery[20] of their liveries; or in the goodly furniture[21] of their horses and armor. But enough of these toys.

12. Round spangles like those now used on Christmas trees. 13. Spangles. 14. Comic performances before or between the acts of a serious masque, used as a contrast to it. 15. Turks. 16. In the serious masque. 17. Jousts: combats between two knights with lances on horseback. 18. A tournament or series of jousts. 19. Mock duels with short swords. 20. Showiness. 21. Equipment.

XXXVIII. OF NATURE IN MEN

Nature is often hidden; sometimes overcome; seldom extinguished. Force maketh nature more violent in the return; doctrine and discourse maketh nature less importune;[1] but custom only doth alter and subdue nature. He that seeketh victory over his nature, let him not set himself too great nor too small tasks, for the first will make him dejected by often failings, and the second will make him a small proceeder, though by often prevailings. And at the first let him practise with helps, as swimmers do with bladders or rushes, but after a time let him practise with disadvantages, as dancers do with 10
thick shoes. For it breeds great perfection, if the practice be harder than the use. Where nature is mighty, and therefore the victory hard, the degrees had need be, first to stay and arrest nature in time, like to him that would say over the four and twenty letters[2] when he was angry; then to go less in quantity, as if one should, in forbearing wine, come from drinking healths to a draught at a meal; and lastly, to discontinue altogether. But if a man have the fortitude and resolution to enfranchise himself at once, that is the best:

Optimus ille animi vindex lædentia pectus 20
Vincula qui rupit, dedoluitque semel.

[He is the best liberator of the mind who snaps the chains which gall his breast and is at once free from grieving].

Neither is the ancient rule amiss, to bend nature as a wand to a contrary extreme, whereby to set it right, understanding it, where the contrary extreme is no vice. Let not a man force a habit upon himself with a perpetual continuance, but with some intermission. For both the pause reinforceth the new onset, and if a man that is not perfect be ever in practice, he shall as well practise his errors as his abilities, and induce 30
one habit of both, and there is no means to help this but by seasonable intermissions. But let not a man trust his victory over his nature too far, for nature will lay[3] buried a great time, and yet revive upon the occasion or temptation. Like as it was with Æsop's damsel, turned from a cat to a woman,

1. Troublesome. 2. Letters of the alphabet. See XXVII, n. 30. 3. Lie.

who sat very demurely at the board's end till a mouse ran before her. Therefore let a man either avoid the occasion altogether, or put himself often to it, that he may be little moved with it. A man's nature is best perceived in privateness, for
40 there is no affectation; in passion, for that putteth a man out of his precepts; and in a new case or experiment, for there custom leaveth him. They are happy men whose natures sort with [4] their vocations; otherwise they may say, *multum incola fuit anima mea* [My soul has long been a sojourner], when they converse [5] in those things they do not affect.[6] In studies, whatsoever a man commandeth upon himself, let him set hours for it; but whatsoever is agreeable to his nature, let him take no care for any set times, for his thoughts will fly to it of themselves, so as [7] the spaces of other business or studies
50 will suffice. A man's nature runs either to herbs or weeds; therefore let him seasonably water the one, and destroy the other.

XXXIX. OF CUSTOM AND EDUCATION

Men's thoughts are much according to their inclination, their discourse and speeches according to their learning and infused opinions, but their deeds are after as [1] they have been accustomed. And therefore, as Machiavel [2] well noteth (though in an evil-favored [3] instance), there is no trusting to the force of nature nor to the bravery [4] of words, except it be corroborate [5] by custom. His instance is, that for the achieving of a desperate conspiracy a man should not rest [6] upon the fierceness of any man's nature or his resolute undertakings,
10 but take such an one as hath had his hands formerly in blood. But Machiavel knew not of a Friar Clement,[7] nor a Ravillac,[8] nor a Jaureguy, nor a Baltazar Gerard; [9] yet his rule holdeth still that nature, nor the engagement of words are not so

4. Suit. 5. Associate. 6. Desire. 7. That. 1. Their deeds conform to what they have been accustomed to. 2. Italian political writer, d. 1527. 3. Ugly. 4. Finery; showiness. 5. Confirmed. 6. Depend. 7. Assassinated Henry III of France in 1589. 8. Killed Henry IV of France in 1610. 9. Jaureguy tried to assassinate William of Orange in 1582, and Gerard did so two years later.

forcible as custom. Only superstition is now so well advanced, that men of the [10] first blood are as firm as butchers by occupation, and votary [11] resolution is made equipollent to custom even in matter of blood. In other things the predominancy of custom is everywhere visible; insomuch as a man would wonder to hear men profess, protest, engage, give great words, and then do just as they have done before, as if they were dead images and engines moved only by the wheels of custom. We see also the reign or tyranny of custom, what it is. The Indians (I mean the sect [12] of their wise men) lay themselves quietly upon a stack of wood, and so sacrifice themselves by fire. Nay the wives strive to be burned with the corpses of their husbands. The lads of Sparta of ancient time were wont to be scourged upon the altar of Diana, without so much as queching.[13] I remember, in the beginning of Queen Elizabeth's time of England, an Irish rebel condemned, put up a petition to the deputy that he might be hanged in a withe, and not in an halter, because it had been so used with former rebels. There be monks in Russia, for penance, that will sit a whole night in a vessel of water, till they be engaged with hard ice. Many examples may be put of the force of custom both upon mind and body. Therefore, since custom is the principal magistrate of man's life, let men by all means endeavor to obtain good customs. Certainly custom is most perfect when it beginneth in young years: this we call education, which is, in effect, but an early custom. So we see, in languages the tongue is more pliant to all expressions and sounds, the joints are more supple to all feats of activity and motions in youth than afterwards. For it is true that late learners cannot so well take the ply,[14] except it be in some minds that have not suffered themselves to fix, but have kept themselves open and prepared to receive continual amendment, which is exceeding rare. But if the force of custom simple and separate be great, the force of custom copulate and conjoined and collegiate [15] is far greater. For there example teacheth, company comforteth,[16] emulation quickeneth, glory raiseth, so as in such places the force of custom is in his exaltation.[17] Certainly the great

10. Who have shed their. 11. Based on a vow. 12. The Gymnosophists or "naked philosophers" of India who considered that clothes hindered purity of thought. 13. Flinching. 14. Be pliant. 15. Joined in one body. 16. Strengthens. 17. Zenith; i.e., able to exert its greatest influence.

multiplication of virtues upon human nature resteth upon societies well ordained and disciplined. For commonwealths and good governments do nourish virtue grown, but do not much mend the seeds. But the misery is that the most effectual means are now applied to the ends least to be desired.

XL. OF FORTUNE

It cannot be denied, but outward accidents conduce much to fortune: favor, opportunity, death of others, occasion[1] fitting virtue.[2] But chiefly, the mould of a man's fortune is in his own hands. *Faber quisque fortunæ suæ* [Every man is the architect of his own fortune], saith the poet. And the most frequent of external causes is that the folly of one man is the fortune of another, for no man prospers so suddenly as by others' errors. *Serpens nisi serpentem comederit non fit draco* [A serpent must swallow a serpent before it can be-
10 come a dragon]. Overt and apparent[3] virtues bring forth praise, but there be secret and hidden virtues that bring forth fortune: certain deliveries[4] of a man's self, which have no name. The Spanish name, *desemboltura* [confident and easy expression], partly expresseth them, when there be not stonds[5] nor restiveness in a man's nature, but that the wheels of his mind keep way with the wheels of his fortune. For so Livy[6] (after he had described Cato Major in these words, *In illo viro tantum robur corporis et animi fuit, ut quocunque loco natus esset, fortunam sibi facturus videretur* [Such was his
20 strength of body and mind, that wherever his birthplace, he could have made himself a fortune]) falleth upon that, that he had *versatile ingenium* [a versatile nature]. Therefore if a man look sharply and attentively, he shall see Fortune, for though she be blind, yet she is not invisible. The way of fortune is like the Milken Way in the sky, which is a meeting or knot of a number of small stars, not seen asunder but giving light together. So are there a number of little and scarce discerned virtues, or rather faculties and customs, that make men fortunate. The Italians note some of them, such as a man

1. Opportunity. 2. Talents. 3. Conspicuous. 4. Disclosures. 5. Hindrances. 6. Roman historian, d. 17 A.D.

would little think. When they speak of one that cannot do amiss, they will throw in into his other conditions, that he hath *Poco di matto* [a little of the fool]. And certainly there be not two more fortunate properties than to have a little of the fool and not too much of the honest. Therefore extreme lovers of their country or masters were never fortunate, neither can they be. For when a man placeth his thoughts without himself, he goeth not his own way. An hasty fortune maketh an enterpriser [7] and remover [8] (the French hath it better, *entreprenant,* or *remuant*), but the exercised [9] fortune maketh the able man. Fortune is to be honored and respected and it be but for [10] her daughters, Confidence and Reputation, for those two Felicity breedeth: the first within a man's self, the latter in others towards him. All wise men, to decline [11] the envy of their own virtues, use to ascribe them to Providence and Fortune, for so they may the better assume them; and besides, it is greatness in a man to be the care of the higher powers. So Cæsar said to the pilot in the tempest, *Cæsarem portas, et fortunam ejus* [You carry Cæsar and his fortune]. So Sylla chose the name of *Felix* [the Fortunate], and not of *Magnus* [the Great]. And it hath been noted that those who ascribe openly too much to their own wisdom and policy end infortunate. It is written that Timotheus the Athenian, after he had, in the account he gave to the state of his government, often interlaced this speech, "and in this Fortune had no part," never prospered in any thing he undertook afterwards. Certainly there be, whose fortunes are like Homer's verses, that have a slide and easiness more than the verses of other poets, as Plutarch saith of Timoleon's [12] fortune, in respect of that of Agesilaus [12] or Epaminondas.[12] And that this should be, no doubt it is much in a man's self.

7. Adventurer. 8. Bustler. 9. Based on experience and use. 10. If it is only for the sake of. 11. Avoid. 12. Greek general, 4th century B.C.

XLI. OF USURY[1]

Many have made witty invectives against usury. They say that it is pity the devil should have God's part, which is the tithe; that the usurer is the greatest Sabbath-breaker, because his plow goeth every Sunday; that the usurer is the drone that Virgil speaketh of:

Ignavuum fucos pecus a præsepibus arcent

[They drive the lazy swarm of drones from the hive]; that the usurer breaketh the first law that was made for mankind after the fall,[2] which was, *In sudore vultus tui comedes*
10 *panem tuum* [In the sweat of thy face shalt thou eat bread], not, *in sudore vultus alieni* [in the sweat of another's face]; that usurers should have orange-tawney bonnets[3] because they do judaize;[4] that it is against nature for money to beget money; and the like. I say this only; that usury is a *concessum propter duritiem cordis* [a concession on account of hardness of heart];[5] for since there must be borrowing and lending, and men are so hard of heart as[6] they will not lend freely, usury must be permitted. Some others have made suspicious and cunning propositions of banks, discovery of men's estates,
20 and other inventions;[7] but few have spoken of usury usefully. It is good to set before us the incommodities and commodities[8] of usury, that the good may be either weighed out or culled out; and warily to provide that while we make forth to that which is better we meet not with that which is worse.

The discommodities of usury are, first, that it makes fewer merchants; for were it not for this lazy trade of usury, money would not lie still, but it would in great part be employed upon merchandising, which is the *vena porta* [the great vein] of wealth in a State. The second, that it makes poor merchants;
30 for as a farmer cannot husband his ground so well if he sit[9]

1. Interest on money, not exorbitant or unlawful interest. 2. The fall of man in the Garden of Eden; *Genesis* iii, 19. 3. Medieval laws commonly required Jews to wear yellow head-dresses. 4. Lend money at interest. In the Middle Ages the chief money-lenders were Jews. 5. See *Matthew* xix, 27. 6. That. 7. Some others have made ingenious representations, based on suspicion, concerning banks, disclosures of men's estates and incomes, and other findings. 8. Disadvantages and advantages. 9. Is settled, or has contracted to pay.

at a great rent, so the merchant cannot drive his trade so well if he sit at great usury. The third is incident to the other two; and that is the decay of customs of kings or estates,[10] which ebb or flow with merchandising. The fourth, that it bringeth the treasure of a realm or state into a few hands; for the usurer being at certainties, and the other at uncertainties, at the end of the game most of the money will be in the box; [11] and ever a state flourisheth when wealth is more equally spread. The fifth, that it beats down the price of land; for the employment of money is chiefly either merchandising or purchasing, and usury waylays both. The sixth, that it doth dull and damp all industries, improvements, and new inventions, wherein money would be stirring if it were not for this slug. The last, that it is the canker and ruin of many men's estates, which in process of time breeds a public poverty. 40

On the other side, the commodities of usury are, first, that howsoever usury in some respects hindereth merchandising, yet in some other it advanceth it, for it is certain that the greatest part of trade is driven by young merchants upon borrowing at interest; so as [12] if the usurer either call in or keep back his money, there will ensue presently a great stand of trade. The second is, that were it not for this easy borrowing upon interest, men's necessities would draw upon them a most sudden undoing, in that they would be forced to sell their means (be it lands or goods) far under foot; [13] and so, whereas usury doth but gnaw upon them, bad markets would swallow them quite up. As for mortgaging or pawning, it will little mend the matter; for either men will not take pawns without use,[14] or if they do, they will look precisely for the forfeiture. I remember a cruel monied man in the country, that would say, "The devil take this usury, it keeps us from forfeitures of mortgages and bonds." The third and last is that it is a vanity to conceive that there would be ordinary borrowing without profit, and it is impossible to conceive the number of inconveniences that will ensue if borrowing be cramped. Therefore, to speak of the abolishing of usury is idle; all states have ever had it in one kind or rate or other—so as that opinion must be sent to Utopia.[15] 50 60

To speak now of the reformation and reglement [16] of

10. States. 11. In the usurer's money-box. 12. So that. 13. Under value. 14. Interest. 15. Imaginary country described by Sir Thomas More, where there was neither private property nor usury. 16. Regulation.

70 usury: how the discommodities of it may be best avoided and the commodities retained. It appears by the balance of commodities and discommodities of usury, two things are to be reconciled: the one, that the tooth of usury be grinded, that[17] it bite not too much; the other, that there be left open a means to invite monied men to lend to the merchants for the continuing and quickening of trade. This cannot be done except you introduce two several sorts of usury, a less and a greater; for if you reduce usury to one low rate, it will ease the common borrower, but the merchant will be to seek for money; and it 80 is to be noted, that the trade of merchandise being the most lucrative, may bear usury at a good rate—other contracts not so.

To serve both intentions, the way would be briefly thus:—that there be two rates of usury: the one, free and general for all; the other, under licence only to certain persons and in certain places of merchandising. First, therefore, let usury in general be reduced to five in the hundred,[18] and let that rate be proclaimed to be free and current, and let the State shut itself out to take[19] any penalty for the same. This will preserve 90 borrowing from any general stop or dryness—this will ease infinite borrowers in the country—this will, in good part, raise the price of land, because land purchased at sixteen years' purchase will yield six in the hundred, and somewhat more; whereas this rate of interest yields but five—this, by like reason, will encourage and edge industrious and profitable improvements, because many will rather venture in that kind than take five in the hundred, especially having been used to greater profit. Secondly, let there be certain persons licensed to lend to known merchants upon usury at a higher rate, and 100 let it be with the cautions following. Let the rate be, even with the merchant himself, somewhat more easy than that he used formerly to pay; for by that means all borrowers shall have some ease by this reformation, be he merchant or whosoever. Let it be no bank or common stock, but every man be master of his own money—not that I altogether mislike banks, but they will hardly be brooked, in regard of[20] certain suspicions. Let the state be answered[21] some small matter for the license, and the rest left to the lender; for if the abatement be but small, it will no whit discourage the lender; for he, for ex-

17. So that. 18. Five per cent. 19. From taking. 20. On account of. 21. Paid.

ample, that took before ten or nine in the hundred, will sooner descend to eight in the hundred than give over this trade of usury and go from certain gains to gains of hazard. Let these licensed lenders be in number indefinite, but restrained to certain principal cities and towns of merchandising; for then they will be hardly able to color [22] other men's monies in the country; so as [23] the license of nine will not suck away the current rate of five, for no man will lend his monies far off, nor put them into unknown hands. 110

If it be objected that this doth in any sort authorize usury, which before was in some places but permissive, the answer is that it is better to mitigate usury by declaration than to suffer it to rage by connivance. 120

XLII. OF YOUTH AND AGE

A man that is young in years may be old in hours, if he have lost no time. But that happeneth rarely. Generally, youth is like the first cogitations, not so wise as the second. For there is a youth in thoughts, as well as in ages. And yet the invention of young men is more lively than that of old, and imaginations stream into their minds better, and as it were more divinely. Natures that have much heat and great and violent desires and perturbations are not ripe for action till they have passed the meridian of their years, as it was with Julius Cæsar and Septimius Severus,[1] of the latter of whom it is said, *Juventutem egit erroribus, imo furoribus, plenam* [He passed a youth full of folly, nay rather of madness]. And yet he was the ablest emperor, almost, of all the list. But reposed [2] natures may do well in youth, as it is seen in Augustus Cæsar,[3] Cosmus Duke of Florence, Gaston de Foix,[4] and others. On the other side, heat and vivacity in age is an excellent composition [5] for business. Young men are fitter to invent than to judge, fitter for execution than for counsel, and fitter for new projects than for settled business; for the experience of age, in things that fall within the compass of it, directeth them, but in new things 10 20

22. Pass for their own. 23. As a result. 1. Roman emperor, d. 211. 2. Calm. 3. Roman emperor. 4. Commander of French armies in Italy, killed 1512. 5. Temperament.

abuseth [6] them. The errors of young men are the ruin of busi ness; but the errors of aged men amount but to this, that mor might have been done, or sooner. Young men, in the conduc and manage of actions, embrace more than they can hold; sti more than they can quiet; fly to the end, without consideratior of the means and degrees; pursue some few principles whicl they have chanced upon absurdly; [7] care not to innovate,[8] which draws unknown inconveniences; use extreme remedie at first; and, that which doubleth all errors, will not acknowl edge or retract them; like an unready horse that will neithe stop nor turn. Men of age object too much, consult too long adventure too little, repent too soon, and seldom drive busines home to the full period,[9] but content themselves with a medi ocrity of success. Certainly it is good to compound employ ments of both; for that will be good for the present, becaus the virtues of either age may correct the defects of both; an good for succession, that young men may be learners whil men in age are actors; and, lastly, good for extern [10] accidents because authority followeth old men, and favor and popular ity youth. But for the moral part, perhaps youth will have th pre-eminence, as age hath for the politic. A certain rabbin,[11] upon the text, "Your young men shall see visions, and you old men shall dream dreams," inferreth that young men ar admitted nearer to God than old, because vision is a cleare revelation than a dream. And certainly, the more a man drink eth of the world, the more it intoxicateth; and age doth profi rather in the powers of understanding, than in the virtues o the will and affections. There be some have [12] an over-earl ripeness in their years, which fadeth betimes. These are, first such as have brittle wits, the edge whereof is soon turned; [13] such as was Hermogenes the rhetorician,[14] whose books are exceeding subtle, who afterwards waxed stupid. A second sort is of those that have some natural dispositions which have bet ter grace in youth than in age, such as is a fluent and luxuriant speech, which becomes youth well, but not age: so Tully [15] saith of Hortensius,[16] *Idem manebat, neque idem decebat*

6. Misdirects. 7. Unseasonably or perversely. In the Latin this word goes with "pursue." 8. Are not careful when they innovate. 9. To completion. 10. External. 11. Rabbi. 12. Who have. 13. Intellects, whose sharpness is soon blunted. 14. Greek rhetorician of the 2nd century, who lost his memory at the age of twenty-five. 15. The Roman orator, Cicero. 16. Roman orator, once a rival of Cicero.

[He remained the same when the same was no longer becoming]. The third is of such as take too high a strain at the first, and are magnanimous more than tract of years can uphold. As was Scipio Africanus,[17] of whom Livy saith in effect, *Ultima primis cedebant* [His end did not match his beginning]. 60

XLIII. OF BEAUTY

Virtue [1] is like a rich stone, best plain set; and surely virtue is best in a body that is comely, though not of delicate features, and that hath rather dignity of presence than beauty of aspect. Neither is it almost [2] seen, that very beautiful persons are otherwise of great virtue,[3] as if nature were rather busy not to err, than in labor to produce excellency. And therefore they prove accomplished, but not of great spirit; [4] and study rather behavior than virtue. But this holds not always: for Augustus Cæsar, Titus Vespasianus,[5] Philip le Bel of France,[6] Edward the Fourth of England, Alcibiades [7] of Athens, Ismael 10 the Sophy of Persia,[8] were all high and great spirits, and yet the most beautiful men of their times. In beauty, that of favor [9] is more [10] than that of color, and that of decent [11] and gracious [12] motion more than that of favor. That is the best part of beauty which a picture cannot express; no nor the first sight of the life.[13] There is no excellent beauty that hath not

17. Roman general, d. 183 B.C. He was better suited for war than for the peaceful times of his later life. 1. Mental and moral excellence, in a broader sense than is common today. Virtue was often viewed as internal beauty, and beauty as outward virtue. B. is interested in the connection of conduct and moral excellence with physical beauty. 2. Generally. 3. I.e., external beauty does not ordinarily co-exist with virtue or internal beauty. 4. Accomplished in external things, but not great or beautiful internally. 5. Roman emperors. 6. Philip IV, the Handsome, king of France, d. 1314. 7. Athenian general and politician, d. 404 B.C. 8. Founder of the Savafid dynasty and first Shah or Sophy of Persia (Iran); d. 1524. 9. General appearance, especially in features, countenance and figure. 10. Better. 11. Becoming, appropriate. 12. Graceful. 13. Which cannot be observed immediately when the living original is seen (because becoming and graceful motion, which is the best part of beauty, cannot be noted at a glance).

some strangeness[14] in the proportion. A man cannot tell whether Apelles[15] or Albert Durer[16] were the more trifler; whereof the one[17] would make a personage by geometrical
20 proportions; the other, by taking the best parts out of divers[18] faces, to make one excellent. Such personages, I think, would please nobody but the painter that made them. Not but I think a painter may make a better face than ever was, but he must do it by a kind of felicity[19] (as a musician that maketh an excellent air in music), and not by rule. A man shall see faces, that if you examine them part by part, you shall find never a good; and yet altogether do well. If it be true that the principal part of beauty is in decent motion, certainly it is no marvel though persons in years seem many times[20] more amiable;
30 *pulchrorum autumnus pulcher* [the autumn of the beautiful is beautiful]; for no youth can be comely but by pardon, and considering the youth as to make up the comeliness.[21] Beauty is as summer fruits, which are easy to corrupt, and cannot last; and for the most part it makes a dissolute youth, and an age a little out of countenance; but yet certainly again, if it light well,[22] it maketh virtue shine, and vices blush.

14. B. probably does not mean *ugliness, an irrational element, something mysterious or inexplicable,* or *distortion.* The Latin text indicates that in the composition of excellent beauty there is something which is less consistent or coherent with other elements than those elements are with each other. I.e., if gracious motion is the best part of beauty, then the proportions of a figure in action necessarily vary from normal static ones; therefore gracious motion inevitably involves some strangeness in proportion. 15. Greek painter, 4th century B.C., erroneously named instead of Zeuxis, an earlier artist. 16. German engraver and painter, d. 1528. His engraving, *Adam and Eve* exemplifies his effort to construct figures geometrically. 17. Dürer. 18. Several. 19. I.e., creative imagination. 20. Many times seem. 21. I.e., youths may have beauty of color and general appearance, but their lack of graceful motion has to be pardoned, unless youth itself is regarded as an excuse for awkwardness. 22. If it alight on a worthy person.

XLIV. OF DEFORMITY

Deformed persons are commonly even with nature; for as nature hath done ill by them, so do they by nature, being for the most part (as the Scripture saith) "void of natural affection"; and so they have their revenge of nature.[1] Certainly there is a consent[2] between the body and the mind, and "where nature erreth in the one she ventureth in the other": *Ubi peccat in uno, periclitatur in altero.* But because there is in man an election[3] touching the frame of his mind, and a necessity in the frame of his body, the stars of natural inclination are sometimes obscured by the sun of discipline and virtue; therefore it is good to consider of deformity, not as a sign which is more deceivable,[4] but as a cause which seldom faileth of the effect. Whosoever hath anything fixed in his person that doth induce contempt hath also a perpetual spur in himself to rescue and deliver himself from scorn; therefore, all deformed persons are extreme bold—first, as in their own defense, as being exposed to scorn; but in process of time, by a general habit. Also, it stirreth in them industry, and especially of this kind, to watch and observe the weakness of others, that they may have somewhat to repay. Again, in their superiors, it quencheth jealousy towards them, as persons that they think they may at pleasure despise; and it layeth their competitors and emulators asleep, as never believing they should be in possibility of advancement, till they see them in possession; so that upon the matter,[5] in a great wit[6] deformity is an advantage to rising. Kings, in ancient times (and at this present, in some countries), were wont to put great trust in eunuchs, because they that are envious towards all are obnoxious and officious[7] towards one; but yet their trust towards them hath rather been as to good spials[8] and good whisperers than good magistrates and officers; and much like is the reason[9] of deformed persons. Still the ground is,[10] they will, if they be

1. "Then since the Heavens have shaped my body so,
Let Hell make crook't my mind to answer it."
Shakespeare, *Richard III.*

2. Agreement. 3. Choice. 4. Deceptive. 5. On the whole. 6. Intellect. 7. Submissive and dutiful. 8. Spies. 9. Rule; ordinary condition. 10. The reason why kings treat eunuchs and deformed persons in this manner remains unchanged; it is that.

of spirit, seek to free themselves from scorn, which must be either by virtue or malice;[11] and therefore, let it not be marveled[12] if sometimes they prove excellent persons; as was Agesilaus,[13] Zanger[14] the son of Solyman, Æsop,[15] Gasca, president of Peru;[16] and Socrates[17] may go likewise amongst them, with others.

XLV. OF BUILDING

Houses are built to live in, and not to look on; therefore let use be preferred before uniformity, except where both may be had. Leave the goodly fabrics of houses, for beauty only, to the enchanted palaces of the poets, who build them with small cost. He that builds a fair house upon an ill seat[1] committeth himself to prison. Neither do I reckon it an ill seat only where the air is unwholesome; but likewise where the air is unequal; as you shall see many fine seats set upon a knap[2] of ground, environed with higher hills round about it, whereby the heat of the sun is pent in and the wind gathereth as in troughs; so as you shall have, and that suddenly, as great diversity of heat and cold as if you dwelt in several places. Neither is it ill air only that maketh an ill seat, but ill ways, ill markets, and, if you will consult with Momus,[3] ill neighbors. I speak not of many more: want of water; want of wood, shade, and shelter; want of fruitfulness, and mixture of grounds of several natures; want of prospect; want of level grounds; want of places at some near distance for sports of hunting, hawking, and races; too near the sea, too remote; having the commodity[4] of navigable rivers, or the discommodity of their overflowing; too far off from great cities, which may hinder

11. Vice. 12. Wondered at. 13. Lame king of Sparta. 14. Son of Solyman the Magnificent, Sultan of Turkey. Zanger was known as the Crooked. 15. An unreliable life of Aesop, reputed author of the famous fables, alleges that he was deformed and ugly. 16. Pedro de la Gasca, d. 1567, a long-limbed Spanish ecclesiastic who put down the rebellion of Pizarro in Peru. 17. This Greek philosopher was ugly but not deformed. 1. Site. 2. Knoll. 3. The Greek god of fault-finding criticized Athena's house because it had no wheels to transport it away from bad neighbors. 4. Convenience. B. seems to have omitted a negative.

business, or too near them, which lurcheth [5] all provisions, and maketh everything dear; where a man hath a great living laid together, and where he is scanted: [6] all which, as it is impossible perhaps to find together, so it is good to know them and think of them, that a man may take as many as he can, and, if he have several dwellings, that he sort [7] them so, that what he wanteth in the one he may find in the other. Lucullus [8] answered Pompey [8] well, who, when he saw his stately galleries and rooms so large and lightsome in one of his houses, 30 said, "Surely an excellent place for summer, but how do you in winter?" Lucullus answered, "Why, do you not think me as wise as some fowl are, that ever change their abode towards the winter?"

To pass from the seat to the house itself, we will do as Cicero doth in the orator's art, who writes books *De Oratore,* and a book he entitles *Orator,* whereof the former delivers the precepts of the art, and the latter the perfection.[9] We will therefore describe a princely palace, making a brief model thereof. For it is strange to see, now in Europe, such huge buildings 40 as the Vatican and Escurial [10] and some others be, and yet scarce a very fair room in them.

First, therefore, I say you cannot have a perfect palace except you have two several [11] sides; a side for the banquet, as is spoken of in the book of Hester,[12] and a side for the houshold, the one for feasts and triumphs,[13] and the other for dwelling. I understand both these sides to be not only returns,[14] but parts of the front, and to be uniform without, though severally partitioned within; and to be on both sides of a great and stately tower in the midst of the front, that, as it were, joineth them 50 together on either hand. I would have on the side of the banquet, in front, one only goodly room above stairs, of some forty foot high, and under it a room for a dressing or preparing place at times of triumphs. On the other side, which is the household side, I wish it divided at the first into a hall and a chapel (with a partition between), both of good state and bigness; and those not to go all the length, but to have at the further end a winter and a summer parlor, both fair. And under these rooms, a fair and large cellar sunk under ground,

5. Takes away. 6. Finds supplies insufficient. 7. Choose. 8. Roman general. 9. Examples of its execution. 10. Edifice near Madrid. 11. Separate. 12. *Esther*. 13. Celebrations and shows. 14. Side wings.

60 and likewise some privy kitchens, with butteries and pantries, and the like. As for the tower, I would have it two stories, of eighteen foot high apiece, above the two wings; and a goodly leads[15] upon the top, railed with statuas interposed; and the same tower to be divided into rooms, as shall be thought fit. The stairs likewise to the upper rooms, let them be upon a fair open newel,[16] and finely railed in with images of wood, cast into a brass color; and a very fair landing-place at the top. But this to be, if you do not point[17] any of the lower rooms for a dining place of servants. For otherwise you shall have the 70 servants' dinner after your own: for the steam of it will come up as in a tunnel. And so much for the front. Only I understand the height of the first stairs to be sixteen foot, which is the height of the lower room.

Beyond this front is there to be a fair court, but three sides of it, of a far lower building than the front. And in all the four corners of that court fair staircases, cast into turrets on the outside and not within the row of buildings themselves. But those towers are not to be of the height of the front, but rather proportionable to the lower building. Let the court not be 80 paved, for that striketh up a great heat in summer and much cold in winter. But only some side alleys,[18] with a cross,[19] and the quarters[20] to graze, being kept shorn, but not too near shorn. The row of return on the banquet side, let it be all stately galleries, in which galleries let there be three or five fine cupolas in the length of it, placed at equal distance, and fine colored windows of several works. On the household side, chambers of presence[21] and ordinary entertainments, with some bed-chambers; and let all three sides be a double house, without thorough[22] lights on the sides, that you may 90 have rooms from the sun, both for forenoon and afternoon. Cast[23] it also, that you may have rooms both for summer and winter, shady for summer, and warm for winter. You shall have sometimes fair houses so full of glass that one cannot tell where to become[24] to be out of the sun or cold. For inbowed[25] windows, I hold them of good use (in cities, in-

15. Leaden strips. 16. Empty column instead of a post in the center of a circular staircase. 17. Appoint. 18. Paths. 19. Path crossing the others. 20. Small areas of turf. 21. For receptions. 22. Windows so arranged that light from them reaches the opposite side of the building. 23. Arrange. 24. Go. 25. Bay.

deed, upright do better, in respect of the uniformity towards the street), for they be pretty retiring places for conference; and besides, they keep both the wind and sun off, for that which would strike almost through the room doth scarce pass the window. But let them be but few, four in the court, on the sides only. 100

Beyond this court, let there be an inward[26] court of the same square and height, which is to be environed with the garden on all sides; and in the inside, cloistered on all sides, upon decent and beautiful arches, as high as the first story. On the under story, towards the garden, let it be turned to a grotto, or place of shade, or estivation.[27] And only have opening and windows towards the garden; and be level upon the floor, no whit sunken under ground, to avoid all dampishness. And let there be a fountain, or some fair work of statuas in 110 the midst of this court; and to be paved as the other court was. These buildings to be for privy lodgings on both sides, and the end for privy galleries. Whereof you must foresee that one of them be for an infirmary, if the prince or any special person should be sick, with chambers, bed-chamber, antecamera,[28] and recamera[29] joining to it. This upon the second story. Upon the ground story, a fair gallery, open, upon pillars; and upon the third story likewise, an open gallery, upon pillars, to take the prospect and freshness of the garden. At both corners of the further side, by way of return, let there be two 120 delicate or rich cabinets,[30] daintily paved, richly hanged, glazed with crystalline glass, and a rich cupola in the midst, and all other elegancy that may be thought upon. In the upper gallery too, I wish that there may be, if the place will yield it, some fountains running in divers places from the wall, with some fine avoidances.[31] And thus much for the model of the palace, save that you must have, before you come to the front, three courts: a green court plain, with a wall about it; a second court of the same, but more garnished, with little turrets, or rather embellishments, upon the wall; and a third court, to 130 make a square with the front, but not to be built, nor yet enclosed with a naked wall, but enclosed with terraces, leaded aloft, and fairly garnished, on the three sides; and cloistered on

26. Inner. 27. Summering. 28. Ante-room. 29. Retiring chamber. 30. Private apartments. 31. Outlets.

the inside, with pillars and not with arches below. As for offices, let them stand at distance, with some low galleries, to pass from them to the palace itself.

XLVI. OF GARDENS

God Almighty first planted a garden. And indeed it is the purest of human pleasures. It is the greatest refreshment to the spirits of man, without which buildings and palaces are but gross handiworks; and a man shall ever see that when ages grow to civility and elegancy, men come to build stately sooner than to garden finely, as if gardening were the greater perfection. I do hold it, in the royal ordering of gardens, there ought to be gardens for all the months in the year, in which severally things of beauty may be then in season. For December and
10 January and the latter part of November, you must take such things as are green all winter: holly, ivy, bays, juniper, cypress-trees, yew, pine-apple-trees,[1] fir-trees; rosemary, lavender; periwinkle, the white, the purple, and the blue; germander,[2] flags; orange-trees, lemon-trees; and myrtles, if they be stoved; [3] and sweet marjoram, warm set.[4] There followeth, for the latter part of January and February, the mezereon-tree,[5] which then blossoms; crocus vernus,[6] both the yellow and the gray, primroses, anemones, the early tulippa, hyacinthus orientalis, chamaïris,[7] fritellaria.[8] For March, there come violets, specially the
20 single blue, which are the earliest; the yellow daffodil, the daisy, the almond-tree in blossom, the peach-tree in blossom, the cornelian-tree in blossom, sweet-briar. In April follow the double white violet, the wall-flower, the stock-gilliflower, the cowslip, flower-de-lices, and lilies of all natures; rosemary-flowers, the tulippa, the double peony, the pale daffodil, the French honeysuckle, the cherry-tree in blossom, the damson and plum-trees in blossom, the white thorn in leaf, the lilac-

1. Pine trees. 2. Mint. 3. Kept warm in a hothouse. 4. Planted in a sunny sheltered place. 5. Small shrub with sweet lilac-colored flowers. 6. Spring crocus. 7. Variety of iris. 8. Lilies with mottled flowers.

tree. In May and June come pinks of all sorts, specially the blush-pink; roses of all kinds, except the musk, which comes later; honeysuckles, strawberries, bugloss, columbine; the French marigold, flos Africanus; cherry-tree in fruit, ribes,[9] figs in fruit, rasps,[10] vine-flowers, lavender in flowers; the sweet satyrian, with the white flower; herba muscaria,[11] lilium convallium,[12] the apple-tree in blossom. In July come gilliflowers of all varieties, musk-roses, the lime-tree in blossom, early pears and plums in fruit, jennetings,[13] codlins.[13] In August come plums of all sorts in fruit, pears, apricots, barberries, filberts, musk-melons, monkshoods of all colors. In September come grapes, apples; poppies of all colors, peaches, melocotones,[14] nectarines,[15] cornelians, wardens,[16] quinces. In October and the beginning of November come services,[17] medlars,[18] bullaces,[19] roses cut or removed [20] to come late, holly-hocks, and such like. These particulars are for the climate of London; but my meaning is perceived, that you may have *ver perpetuum* [perpetual spring], as the place affords.

And because the breath of flowers is far sweeter in the air (where is comes and goes like the warbling of music) than in the hand, therefore nothing is more fit for that delight than to know what be the flowers and plants that do best perfume the air. Roses, damask and red, are fast [21] flowers of their smells, so that you may walk by a whole row of them, and find nothing of their sweetness, yea though it be in a morning's dew. Bays likewise yield no smell as they grow, rosemary little; nor sweet marjoram. That which above all others yields the sweetest smell in the air is the violet, specially the white double violet, which comes twice a year, about the middle of April, and about Bartholomew-tide.[22] Next to that is the musk-rose. Then the strawberry-leaves dying, which [emit] [23] a most excellent cordial smell. Then the flower of the vines; it is a little dust, like the dust of a bent,[24] which grows upon the cluster in the first coming forth. Then sweet-briar. Then wall-flowers, which are very delightful to be set under a parlor or lower

9. Currants and gooseberries. 10. Raspberries. 11. Musk-scented grape hyacinth. 12. Lily of the valley. 13. Early apples. 14. Large peaches. 15. Smooth-skinned peaches. 16. Kind of pears. 17. Shadberries. 18. Fruit like crab apples. 19. Kind of plum. 20. Transplanted. 21. Retentive. 22. Aug. 24, St. Bartholomew's day. 23. A word is missing in the original. 24. Various kinds of grasses.

chamber window. Then pinks and gilliflowers, specially the matted pink and clove gilliflower. Then the flowers of the lime-tree. Then the honeysuckles, so they be somewhat afar off. Of bean-flowers I speak not, because they are field flowers. But those which perfume the air most delightfully, not passed by as the rest, but being trodden upon and crushed, are three: that is, burnet, wild-thyme, and watermints. Therefore you are 70 to set whole alleys [25] of them, to have the pleasure when you walk or tread.

For gardens (speaking of those which are indeed prince-like, as we have done of buildings), the contents ought not well to be under thirty acres of ground; and to be divided into three parts: a green in the entrance; a heath or desert [26] in the going forth; and the main garden in the midst, besides alleys on both sides. And I like well that four acres of ground be assigned to the green, six to the heath, four and four to either side, and twelve to the main garden. The green hath two pleasures: the 80 one, because nothing is more pleasant to the eye than green grass kept finely shorn; the other, because it will give you a fair alley in the midst by which you may go in front upon a stately hedge,[27] which is to enclose the garden. But because the alley will be long, and, in great heat of the year or day, you ought not to buy the shade in the garden by going in the sun through the green; therefore you are, of either side the green, to plant a covert alley upon carpenter's work, about twelve foot in height, by which you may go in shade into the garden. As for the making of knots or figures with divers colored earths, 90 that they may lie under the windows of the house on that side which the garden stands, they be but toys; you may see as good sights many times in tarts. The garden is best to be square, encompassed on all the four sides with a stately arched hedge, the arches to be upon pillars of carpenter's work of some ten foot high and six foot broad, and the spaces between of the same dimension with the breadth of the arch. Over the arches let there be an entire hedge of some four foot high, framed also upon carpenter's work; and upon the upper hedge, over every arch, a little turret, with a belly, enough to receive a cage of 100 birds; and over every space between the arches some other little figure, with broad plates of round colored glass gilt, for the sun

25. Pathways. 26. Ground left in a wild state. 27. Fence; so throughout the essay.

to play upon. But this hedge I intend to be raised upon a bank, not steep, but gently slope,[28] of some six foot, set all with flowers. Also I understand that this square of the garden should not be the whole breadth of the ground, but to leave on either side ground enough for diversity of side alleys, unto which the two covert alleys of the green may deliver you. But there must be no alleys with hedges at either end of this great enclosure; not at the hither end, for letting[29] your prospect upon this fair hedge from the green; nor at the further end, 110 for letting your prospect from the hedge through the arches upon the heath.

For the ordering of the ground within the great hedge, I leave it to variety of device, advising nevertheless that whatsoever form you cast it into, first, it be not too busy[30] or full of work. Wherein I, for my part, do not like images cut out in juniper or other garden stuff; they be for children. Little low hedges, round, like welts,[31] with some pretty pyramids, I like well; and in some places, fair columns upon frames of carpenter's work. I would also have the alleys spacious and fair. 120 You may have closer alleys upon the side grounds, but none in the main garden. I wish also, in the very middle, a fair mount, with three ascents and alleys, enough for four to walk abreast, which I would have to be perfect circles, without any bulwarks or embossments;[32] and the whole mount to be thirty foot high; and some fine banqueting-house, with some chimneys neatly cast, and without too much glass.

For fountains, they are a great beauty and refreshment, but pools mar all and make the garden unwholesome and full of flies and frogs. Fountains I intend to be of two natures: the 130 one that sprinkleth or spouteth water; the other a fair receipt of water, of some thirty or forty foot square, but without fish or slime or mud. For the first, the ornaments of images gilt or of marble, which are in use, do well: but the main matter is so to convey the water, as it never stay either in the bowls or in the cistern; that the water be never by rest discolored, green or red or the like, or gather any mossiness or putrefaction. Besides that, it is to be cleansed every day by the hand. Also some steps up to it and some fine pavement about it doth well. As for the other kind of fountain, which we may call a bath- 140

28. Sloping. 29. Impeding. 30. Complicated. 31. Borders or edges, as of a gown. 32. Protuberances.

ing pool, it may admit much curiosity[33] and beauty, wherewith we will not trouble ourselves: as that the bottom be finely paved, and with images; the sides likewise; and withal embellished with colored glass and such things of luster; encompassed also with fine rails of low statuas. But the main point is the same which we mentioned in the former kind of fountain, which is that the water be in perpetual motion, fed by a water higher than the pool and delivered into it by fair spouts and then discharged away under ground by some equality of
150 bores,[34] that it stay little. And for fine devices of arching water without spilling and making it rise in several forms (of feathers, drinking glasses, canopies, and the like), they be pretty things to look on, but nothing to health and sweetness.

For the heath, which was the third part of our plot, I wish it to be framed, as much as may be, to a natural wildness. Trees I would have none in it, but some thickets made only of sweet-briar and honeysuckle, and some wild vine amongst; and the ground set with violets, strawberries, and primroses; for these are sweet, and prosper in the shade; and these to be in the
160 heath, here and there, not in any order. I like also little heaps, in the nature of mole-hills (such as are in wild heaths), to be set, some with wild thyme; some with pinks; some with germander, that gives a good flower to the eye; some with periwinkle; some with violets; some with strawberries; some with cowslips; some with daisies; some with red roses; some with lilium convallium; some with sweet-williams red; some with bear's-foot: and the like low flowers, being withal sweet and sightly. Part of which heaps are to be with standards[35] of little bushes pricked[36] upon their top, and part without. The
170 standards to be roses, juniper, holly, barberries (but here and there, because of the smell of their blossoms), red currants; gooseberries, rosemary, bays, sweet-briar, and such like. But these standards to be kept with cutting, that they grow not out of course.[37]

For the side grounds, you are to fill them with variety of alleys, private, to give a full shade, some of them, wheresoever the sun be. You are to frame some of them likewise for shelter, that when the wind blows sharp you may walk as in a gallery. And those alleys must be likewise hedged at both ends to keep

33. Elaborateness. 34. Pipes. 35. Stands. 36. Planted. 37. Due limits.

out the wind; and these closer alleys must be ever finely grav- 180
eled, and no grass, because of going wet. In many of these alleys likewise, you are to set fruit-trees of all sorts, as well upon the walls as in ranges. And this would be generally observed, that the borders wherein you plant your fruit-trees be fair and large, and low, and not steep, and set with fine flowers, but thin and sparingly, lest they deceive [38] the trees. At the end of both the side grounds I would have a mount of some pretty height, leaving the wall of the enclosure breast high, to look abroad into the fields.

For the main garden, I do not deny but there should be some 190
fair alleys ranged on both sides with fruit-trees; and some pretty tufts of fruit-trees, and arbors with seats, set in some decent order, but these to be by no means set too thick, but to leave the main garden so as it be not close, but the air open and free. For as for shade, I would have you rest upon the alleys of the side grounds, there to walk, if you be disposed, in the heat of the year or day, but to make account that the main garden is for the more temperate parts of the year, and, in the heat of summer, for the morning and the evening, or overcast days. 200

For aviaries, I like them not, except they be of that largeness as they may be turfed, and have living plants and bushes set in them; that the birds may have more scope and natural nestling, and that no foulness appear in the floor of the aviary. So I have made a platform [39] of a princely garden, partly by precept, partly by drawing, not a model, but some general lines of it, and in this I have spared for no cost. But it is nothing for great princes, that for the most part taking advice with workmen, with no less cost set their things together; and sometimes add statuas and such things for state and magnificence, but 210
nothing to the true pleasure of a garden.

38. Cheat of nutriment. 39. Plan.

XLVII. OF NEGOTIATING

It is generally better to deal by speech than by letter, and by the mediation of a third than by a man's self. Letters are good when a man would draw an answer by letter back again, or when it may serve for a man's justification afterwards to produce his own letter, or where it may be danger to be interrupted or heard by pieces. To deal in person is good when a man's face breedeth regard, as commonly with inferiors, or in tender[1] cases, where a man's eye upon the countenance of him with whom he speaketh may give him a direction how far to
10 go; and generally, where a man will reserve to himself liberty either to disavow or to expound. In choice of instruments, it is better to choose men of a plainer sort, that are like to do that that is committed to them, and to report back again faithfully the success, than those that are cunning[2] to contrive out of other men's business somewhat to grace themselves, and will help the matter in report for satisfaction sake. Use also such persons as affect[3] the business wherein they are employed, for that quickeneth much; and such as are fit for the matter, as bold men for expostulation, fair-spoken men for persuasion,
20 crafty men for inquiry and observation, froward and absurd[4] men for business that doth not well bear out itself.[5] Use also such as have been lucky, and prevailed before in things wherein you have employed them; for that breeds confidence, and they will strive to maintain their prescription.[6] It is better to sound a person with whom one deals afar off, than to fall upon the point at first, except[7] you mean to surprise him by some short question. It is better dealing with men in appetite,[8] than with those that are where they would be. If a man deal with another upon conditions, the start or first performance
30 is all,[9] which a man cannot reasonably demand, except[7] either the nature of the thing be such which must go before, or else[7] a man can persuade the other party that he shall still need him in some other thing, or else[7] that he be counted the hon-

1. Delicate. 2. Know how. 3. Like. 4. Foolish, perverse. 5. That will not bear close examination (because it is unjust). 6. Priority rights for such employment. 7. Unless. 8. With a desire for advancement. 9. All-important.

ester man. All practice is to discover or to work.[10] Men discover themselves in trust, in passion, at unawares, and of necessity, when they would have somewhat done and cannot find an apt pretext. If you would work any man, you must either know his nature and fashions,[11] and so lead him; or his ends, and so persuade him; or his weakness and disadvantages, and so awe him; or those that have interest in him, and so govern him. In dealing with cunning persons, we must ever consider their ends, to interpret their speeches; and it is good to say little to them, and that which they least look for. In all negotiations of difficulty, a man may not look to sow and reap at once; but must prepare business, and so ripen it by degrees. 40

XLVIII. OF FOLLOWERS AND FRIENDS

Costly followers[1] are not to be liked, lest while a man maketh his train longer, he make his wings shorter. I reckon to be costly not them alone which charge the purse, but which are wearisome and importune in suits. Ordinary followers ought to challenge no higher conditions than countenance, recommendation and protection from wrongs. Factious followers are worse to be liked, which follow not upon affection to him with whom they range themselves, but upon discontentment conceived against some other; whereupon commonly ensueth that ill intelligence[2] that we many times see between great personages. Likewise glorious[3] followers, who make themselves as trumpets of the commendation of those they follow, are full of inconvenience, for they taint business through want of secrecy, and they export honor from a man and make him a return in envy. There is a kind of followers likewise which are dangerous, being indeed espials,[4] which inquire the secrets of the house, and bear tales of them to others. Yet such men, many times, are in great favor, for they are officious,[5] 10

10. The purpose of all clever dealing is to find out things about men or to make use of them. 11. Habits. 1. Servants or hangers-on. 2. Misunderstanding. 3. Boastful. 4. Spies. 5. Energetic and punctilious in the performance of their work.

and commonly exchange tales. The following by certain
20 estates[6] of men, answerable[7] to that which a great person
himself professeth (as of soldiers to him that hath been employed in the wars, and the like), hath ever been a thing civil,[8]
and well taken even in monarchies; so it be without too much
pomp or popularity. But the most honorable kind of following
is to be followed as one that apprehendeth[9] to advance virtue
and desert in all sorts of persons. And yet, where there is no
eminent odds in sufficiency,[10] it is better to take with the
more passable,[11] than with the more able. And besides, to
speak truth, in base times active men are of more use than
30 virtuous.[12] It is true that in government it is good to use men
of one rank equally, for to countenance some extraordinarily
is to make them insolent and the rest discontent, because they
may claim a due. But contrariwise, in favor, to use men with
much difference and election is good, for it maketh the persons
perferred more thankful, and the rest more officious, because
all is of favor.[13] It is good discretion not to make too much of
any man at the first, because one cannot hold out that proportion. To be governed (as we call it) by one is not safe, for it
shows softness and gives a freedom to scandal and disreputa-
40 tion,[14] for those that would not censure or speak ill of a man
immediately will talk more boldly of those that are so great
with them, and thereby wound their honor. Yet to be distracted with many is worse, for it makes men to be of the
last impression, and full of change. To take advice of some
few friends is ever honorable; "for lookers-on many times see
more than gamesters; and the vale best discovereth the hill."
There is little friendship in the world, and least of all between
equals, which was wont to be magnified.[15] That that is, is
between superior and inferior, whose fortunes may compre-
50 hend[16] the one the other.

6. Ranks or classes. 7. Equivalent or similar. 8. Seemly. 9. A person who intends. 10. Outstanding difference in ability. 11. Mediocre, ordinary. 12. Used in a broad sense. B. clearly refers more to ability and talents than to morals. 13. Of graciousness (not obligation). 14. Disrepute. 15. Praised highly or exaggerated (by ancient writers). 16. Include.

L. OF STUDIES

Studies[1] serve for delight, for ornament, and for ability. Their chief use for delight is in privateness and retiring;[2] for ornament, is in discourse; and for ability, is in the judgment and disposition of business. For expert[3] men can execute, and perhaps judge of particulars, one by one; but the general counsels, and the plots and marshaling of affairs come best from those that are learned. To spend too much time in studies is sloth; to use them too much for ornament, is affectation; to make judgment wholly by their rules, is the humor[4] of a scholar. They perfect nature, and are perfected by experience, for natural abilities are like natural plants that need pruning by study; and studies themselves do give forth directions too much at large, except they be bounded in by experience. Crafty men contemn studies, simple men admire them, and wise men use them; for they teach not their own use, but that is a wisdom without them and above them, won by observation. Read not to contradict and confute; nor to believe and take for granted; nor to find talk and discourse; but to weigh and consider. Some books are to be tasted, others to be swallowed, and some few to be chewed and digested; that is, some books are to be read only in parts; others to be read, but not curiously;[5] and some few to be read wholly and with diligence and attention. Some books also may be read by deputy, and extracts made of them by others, but that would[6] be only in the less important arguments and the meaner sort of books; else distilled books are like common distilled waters, flashy[7] things. Reading maketh a full man; conference a ready man; and writing an exact man. And therefore, if a man write little, he had need have a great memory; if he confer little, he had need have a present wit: and if he read little, he had need have much cunning, to seem to know that he doth not. Histories make men wise, poets witty,[8] the mathematics

1. Used in a broad sense, including reading. 2 Privacy and retirement. 3. Experienced in practical affairs (but with little book-learning). 4. Eccentricity. 5. Attentively. 6. Should. 7. Insipid or specious. 8. Wise, ingenious.

subtile, natural philosophy deep, moral grave, logic and rhetoric able to contend. *Abeunt studia in mores* [Studies are transformed into manners]. Nay, there is no stond[9] or impediment in the wit[10] but may be wrought out by fit studies, like as diseases of the body may have appropriate exercises. Bowling is good for the stone[11] and reins,[12] shooting for the lungs and breast; gentle walking for the stomach; riding for
40 the head; and the like. So if a man's wit be wandering, let him study the mathematics; for in demonstrations, if his wit be called away never so little, he must begin again. If his wit be not apt to distinguish or find differences, let him study the Schoolmen,[13] for they are *cymini sectores* [hair-splitters]. If he be not apt to beat over matters,[14] and to call up one thing to prove and illustrate another, let him study the lawyers' cases. So every defect of the mind may have a special receipt.

LI. OF FACTION

Many have an opinion not wise, that for a prince to govern his estate[1] or for a great person to govern his proceedings according to the respect of factions, is a principal part of policy; whereas contrariwise, the chiefest wisdom is either in ordering those things which are general, and wherein men of several[2] factions do nevertheless agree, or in dealing with correspondence[3] to particular persons, one by one. But I say not that the consideration of factions is to be neglected. Mean[4] men, in their rising, must adhere,[5] but great men, that have strength
10 in themselves, were better to maintain themselves indifferent and neutral. Yet even in beginners, to adhere so moderately, as he be a man of the one faction which is most passable with the other,[6] commonly giveth best way. The lower and weaker

9. Obstacle. 10. Mind or intelligence. 11. Bladder or gall-bladder. 12. Kidneys. 13. See XVII, n. 6. 14. Cover the ground thoroughly.
1. State. 2. Different. 3. Adaptation. 4. Ordinary, common. 5. Belong to a faction or party. 6. For a man to adhere so moderately to one faction as to become the man of that party who is most acceptable to the other.

little to keep state. Amongst a man's inferiors one shall be sure of reverence, and therefore it is good a little to be familiar. He that is too much in anything, so that he giveth another 30 occasion of satiety, maketh himself cheap. To apply one's self to others is good, so[6] it be with demonstration that a man doth it upon regard[7] and not upon facility.[8] It is a good precept generally in seconding another, yet to add somewhat of one's own; as,[9] if you will grant his opinion, let it be with some distinction; if you will follow his motion, let it be with condition; if you allow his counsel, let it be with alleging further reason. Men had need beware how they be too perfect in compliments, for, be they never so sufficient otherwise, their enviers will be sure to give them that attribute to the disadvan- 40 tage of their greater virtues. It is loss also in business to be too full of respects or to be curious[10] in observing times and opportunities. Solomon saith, "He that considereth the wind shall not sow, and he that looketh to the clouds shall not reap." A wise man will make more opportunities than he finds. Men's behavior should be like their apparel, not too strait or point device,[11] but free for exercise or motion.

LIII. OF PRAISE

Praise is the reflection of virtue, but it is as the glass or body which giveth the reflection. If it be from the common people, it is commonly false and naught, and rather followeth vain persons than virtuous. For the common people understand not many excellent virtues. The lowest virtues draw praise from them; the middle virtues work in them astonishment or admiration; but of the highest virtues they have no sense of perceiving at all. But shows, and *species virtutibus similes* [appearances resembling virtues] serve best with them. Certainly fame is like a river that beareth up things light and swoln 10 and drowns things weighty and solid. But if persons of quality and judgment concur, then it is (as the Scripture saith)

6. Provided that. 7. Out of consideration for others. 8. Because of a yielding disposition. 9. For example. 10. Too careful. 11. Precise.

nomen bonum instar unguenti fragrantis [a good name is like a sweet ointment]: it filleth all round about, and will not easily away. For the odors of ointments are more durable than those of flowers. There be so many false points of praise, that a man may justly hold it a suspect. Some praises proceed merely of flattery; and if he be an ordinary flatterer, he will have [1] certain common attributes which may serve every man;
20 if he be a cunning flatterer, he will follow the arch-flatterer, which is a man's self, and wherein a man thinketh best of himself, therein the flatterer will uphold him most; but if he be an impudent flatterer, look wherein a man is conscious to himself that he is most defective, and is most out of countenance in himself,[2] that will the flatterer entitle him to perforce, *spreta conscientia* [disdaining conscience]. Some praises come of good wishes and respects, which is a form due in civility to kings and great persons, *laudando præcipere* [to teach by praising], when by telling men what they are, they represent to them
30 what they should be. Some men are praised maliciously to their hurt, thereby to stir envy and jealousy towards them: *pessimum genus inimicorum laudantium* [the worst class of enemies are men that praise], insomuch as it was a proverb amongst the Grecians, that "he that was praised to his hurt should have a push [3] rise upon his nose," as we say, "that a blister will rise upon one's tongue that tells a lie." Certainly moderate praise, used with opportunity, and not vulgar, is that which doth the good. Solomon saith, "He that praiseth his friend aloud, rising early, it shall be to him no better than a curse."
40 Too much magnifying of man or matter doth irritate [4] contradiction, and procure envy and scorn. To praise a man's self cannot be decent,[5] except it be in rare cases, but to praise a man's office or profession, he may do it with good grace and with a kind of magnanimity. The cardinals of Rome, which are theologues [6] and friars and Schoolmen,[7] have a phrase of notable contempt and scorn towards civil business, for they call all temporal business of wars, embassages, judicature, and other employments, "sbirrerie," which is *under-sheriffries,* as if they were but matters for under-sheriffs and catch-poles,[8]

1. He will ascribe (to the man he is flattering). 2. Ashamed of himself. 3. Pimple full of pus. 4. Provoke. 5. Seemly. 6. Theologians. 7. See XVII, n. 6. 8. Bailiff's assistants.

though many times those under-sheriffries do more good than 50
their high speculations. St. Paul, when he boasts of himself, he doth oft interlace, "I speak like a fool," but speaking of his calling, he saith, *magnificabo apostolatum meum* [I will magnify my mission].

LIV. OF VAINGLORY

It was prettily devised of Æsop, "The fly sat upon the axle-tree of the chariot wheel, and said, 'What a dust do I raise!'" So are there some vain persons, that whatsoever goeth alone or moveth upon greater means,[1] if they have never so little hand in it, they think it is they that carry it. They that are glorious[2] must needs be factious, for all bravery[3] stands upon comparisons. They must needs be violent to make good their own vaunts. Neither can they be secret, and therefore not effectual, but according to the French proverb, *Beaucoup de bruit, peu de fruit*: "Much bruit,[4] little fruit." Yet cer- 10
tainly there is use of this quality in civil affairs. Where there is an opinion and fame to be created either of virtue or greatness, these men are good trumpeters. Again, as Titus Livius[5] noteth in the case of Antiochus and the Ætolians,[6] "There are sometimes great effects of cross lies," as if a man that negotiates between two princes to draw them to join in a war against the third, doth extol the forces of either of them above measure, the one to the other; and sometimes he that deals between man and man raiseth his own credit with both by pretending greater interest than he hath in either. And in 20
these and the like kinds, it often falls out that somewhat is produced of nothing, for lies are sufficient to breed opinion, and opinion brings on substance. In militar commanders and soldiers, vain-glory is an essential point, for as iron sharpens iron, so by glory[7] one courage sharpeneth another. In cases of

1. Through other means than the vainglorious person. 2. Boastful. 3. Ostentation. 4. Noise. 5. Roman historian. 6. Antiochus, King of Syria, allied with the Aetolians but was defeated. 7. Boasting.

great enterprise upon charge and adventure,[8] a composition of glorious [9] natures doth put life into business, and those that are of solid and sober natures have more of the ballast than of the sail. In fame of learning, the flight will be slow
30 without some feathers of ostentation. *Qui de contemnenda gloria libros scribunt, nomen suum inscribunt* [Men who write books on the worthlessness of glory put their names on the title page]. Socrates, Aristotle, Galen,[10] were men full of ostentation. Certainly vain-glory helpeth to perpetuate a man's memory, and virtue was never so beholding [11] to human nature, as [12] it received his [13] due at the second hand. Neither had the fame of Cicero, Seneca, Plinius Secundus [14] borne her age [15] so well, if it had not been joined with some vanity in themselves, like unto varnish that makes ceilings not only
40 shine but last. But all this while, when I speak of vain-glory, I mean not of that property that Tacitus doth attribute to Mucianus: [16] *Omnium quæ dixerat feceratque arte quadam ostentator* [With a certain skill, he displayed to advantage everything that he had said and done], for that proceeds not of vanity, but of natural magnanimity and discretion, and in some persons is not only comely, but gracious. For excusations, cessions,[17] modesty itself well governed are but arts of ostentation. And amongst those arts there is none better than that which Plinius Secundus speaketh of, which is to be liberal of
50 praise and commendation to others, in [18] that wherein a man's self hath any perfection. For saith Pliny very wittily,[19] "In commending another you do yourself right, for he that you commend is either superior to you in that you commend, or inferior. If he be inferior, if he be to be commended, you much more; if he be superior, if he be not to be commended, you much less." Glorious men are the scorn of wise men, the admiration of fools, the idols of parasites, and the slaves of their own vaunts.

8. Subject to expense and risk. 9. A combination of boastful. 10. Greek physician, born 131. 11. Indebted. 12. That. 13. Its. 14. Pliny the Younger, Roman writer on rhetoric. 15. Lasted. 16. Three times Roman consul. 17. Concessions. 18. Concerning. 19. Wisely, ingeniously.

LV. OF HONOR AND REPUTATION

The winning of honor is but the revealing of a man's virtue and worth without disadvantage. For some in their actions do woo and affect [1] honor and reputation, which sort of men are commonly much talked of but inwardly little admired. And some, contrariwise, darken their virtue in the show of it, so as [2] they be undervalued in opinion. If a man perform that which hath not been attempted before, or attempted and given over, or hath been achieved, but not with so good circumstance, he shall purchase more honor than by effecting a matter of greater difficulty or virtue, wherein he is but a follower. If a man so temper his actions, as [2] in some one of them he doth content every faction or combination of people, the music will be the fuller. A man is an ill husband [3] of his honor that entereth into any action, the failing wherein may disgrace him more than the carrying of it through can honor him. Honor that is gained and broken upon another [4] hath the quickest [5] reflection, like diamonds cut with facets. And therefore let a man contend to excel any competitors of his in honor, in outshooting them, if he can, in their own bow. Discreet followers and servants help much to reputation. *Omnis fama a domesticis emanat* [All fame proceeds from domestics]. Envy, which is the canker of honor, is best extinguished by declaring [6] a man's self in his ends rather than to seek merit than fame, and by attributing a man's successes rather to divine Providence and felicity, than to his own virtue or policy. The true marshaling of the degrees of sovereign honor are these: In the first place are *conditores imperiorum,* founders of states and commonwealths, such as were Romulus, Cyrus, Cæsar, Ottoman, Ismael.[7] In the second place are *legislatores,* lawgivers, which are also called second founders, or *perpetui principes* [perpetual rulers], because they govern by their ordinances after they are gone; such were Lycurgus, Solon, Justin-

1. Long for. 2. That. 3. Manager. 4. Obtained at another's expense. 5. Liveliest. 6. Revealing. 7. Founders respectively of Rome (according to legend); the Persian empire (6th century B.C.); the Roman empire; the Turkish empire (Osman I, d. 1326); and the Safavid dynasty, rulers of Persia from about 1503.

ian, Eadgar, Alphonsus of Castile, the Wise, that made the *Siete Partidas* [Seven Parts].[8] In the third place are *liberatores,* or *salvatores* [saviors], such as compound the long miseries of civil wars, or deliver their countries from servitude of strangers or tyrants, as Augustus Cæsar,[9] Vespasianus,[10] Aurelianus,[11] Theodoricus,[12] King Henry the Seventh of England,[13] King Henry the Fourth of France.[14] In the fourth
40 place are *propagatores* or *propugnatores imperii* [defenders of the empire]; such as in honorable wars enlarge their territories or make noble defense against invaders. And in the last place are *patres patriæ* [fathers of their country], which reign justly and make the times good wherein they live. Both which last kinds need no examples, they are in such number. Degrees of honor in subjects are, first *participes curarum* [sharers of cares], those upon whom princes do discharge the greatest weight of their affairs, their "right hands," as we call them. The next are *duces belli,* great leaders [in war], such as are
50 princes' lieutenants, and do them notable services in the wars. The third are *gratiosi,* favorites, such as exceed not this scantling,[15] to be solace to the sovereign, and harmless to the people. And the fourth, *negotiis pares* [those who are capable in business]: such as have great places under princes and execute their places with sufficiency. There is an honor, likewise, which may be ranked amongst the greatest, which happeneth rarely; that is, of such as sacrifice themselves to death or danger for the good of their country, as was M. Regulus,[16] and the two Decii.[17]

8. Lawgivers respectively of Sparta, 9th century B.C.; Athens, d. 559 B.C.; the Byzantine empire, 6th century; England, 10th century (He was surnamed "the Peaceful"); and Castile, 13th century (His *Seven Parts* is the basis of Spanish jurisprudence). 9. First Roman emperor; brought peace and security. 10. Roman emperor, 70-79; relieved the empire of civil wars after the death of Nero. 11. Roman emperor, 270-275, called "Restorer of the Roman Empire." 12. Theodoric the Great, 454-526, king of the Ostrogoths who gave 33 years of peace to Italy. 13. Ruled 1485 to 1509; ended the Wars of the Roses and maintained peace. 14. Ruled 1589-1610; ended wars of religion in France. 15. Measure. 16. Roman general, taken prisoner by the Carthaginians in the First Punic War. When sent to Rome to ask for an exchange of prisoners, he persuaded the Senate to refuse, and voluntarily returned to Carthage, where he was put to death about 250 B.C. 17. Publius Decius Mus and his son of the same name were both killed in battles.

LVI. OF JUDICATURE

Judges ought to remember that their office is *jus dicere,* and not *jus dare:* to interpret law, and not to make law or give law. Else will it be like the authority claimed by the Church of Rome, which under pretext of exposition of Scripture doth not stick [1] to add and alter, and to pronounce that which they do not find, and by show of antiquity to introduce novelty. Judges ought to be more learned than witty,[2] more reverend than plausible, [3] and more advised [4] than confident. Above all things, integrity is their portion and proper virtue. "Cursed," saith the law,[5] "is he that removeth the landmark." [6] The mis- 10 layer of the mere-stone [6] is to blame. But it is the unjust judge that is the capital [7] remover of landmarks when he defineth amiss of lands and property. One foul sentence doth more hurt than many foul examples. For these do but corrupt the stream; the other corrupteth the fountain. So saith Solomon, *Fons turbatus, et vena corrupta, est justus cadens in causa sua coram adversario* [A righteous man falling down before the wicked is as a troubled fountain or a corrupt spring]. The office of judges may have reference unto the parties that sue, unto the advocates that plead, unto the clerks and ministers of 20 justice underneath them, and to the sovereign or state above them.

First, for the causes or parties that sue. "There be," saith the Scripture, "that turn judgment into wormwood"; and surely there be also that turn it into vinegar, for injustice maketh it bitter, and delays make it sour. The principal duty of a judge is to suppress force and fraud, whereof force is the more pernicious when it is open, and fraud when it is close and disguised. Add thereto contentious suits, which ought to be spewed out, as the surfeit of courts. A judge ought to prepare 30 his way to a just sentence, as God useth to prepare his way, by raising valleys and taking down hills: so when there appeareth on either side an high hand, violent prosecution, cun-

1. Hesitate. 2. Ingenious. 3. More to be revered than to be applauded. 4. Deliberate. 5. *Deuteronomy* xxvii, 17. The Mosaic law. 6. Boundary stone. 7. Chief.

ning advantages taken, combination, power, great counsel, then is the virtue of a judge seen, to make inequality equal, that he may plant his judgment as upon an even ground. *Qui fortiter emungit, elicit sanguinem* [Violent nose-blowing causes bleeding]; and where the wine-press is hard wrought, it yields a harsh wine that tastes of the grape-stone.
40 Judges must beware of hard constructions and strained inferences, for there is no worse torture [8] than the torture of laws. Specially in case of laws penal, they ought to have care that that which was meant for terror be not turned into rigor, and that they bring not upon the people that shower whereof the Scripture speaketh, *Pluet super eos laqueos* [He shall rain a shower of snares upon them], for penal laws pressed are a "shower of snares" upon the people. Therefore let penal laws, if they have been sleepers of long,[9] or if they be grown unfit for the present time, be by wise judges confined in the execu-
50 tion: *Judicis officium est, ut res, ita tempora rerum, etc.* [It is a judge's duty to consider the time as well as the matter]. In causes of life and death, judges ought (as far as the law permitteth) in justice to remember mercy, and to cast a severe eye upon the example, but a merciful eye upon the person.

Secondly, for the advocates and counsel that plead. Patience and gravity of hearing is an essential part of justice, and an overspeaking judge is no well-tuned cymbal. It is no grace to a judge first to find that which he might have heard in due time
60 from the bar; or to show quickness of conceit [10] in cutting off evidence or counsel too short; or to prevent [11] information by questions, though pertinent. The parts of a judge in hearing are four: to direct the evidence; to moderate length, repetition, or impertinency [12] of speech; to recapitulate, select, and collate the material points of that which hath been said; and to give the rule or sentence. Whatsoever is above these is too much, and proceedeth either of glory [13] and willingness to speak or of impatience to hear or of shortness of memory or of want of a staid and equal [14] attention. It is a strange thing to see that
70 the boldness of advocates should prevail with judges; whereas they should imitate God, in whose seat they sit, who "repress-

8. Wresting, as well as causing pain. 9. Inoperative for a long time. 10. Conception, understanding. 11. Anticipate. 12. Irrelevancy. 13. Vainglory. 14. Equable, steady.

eth the presumptuous," and "giveth grace to the modest." But it is more strange, that judges should have noted favorites; which cannot but cause multiplication of fees, and suspicion of by-ways. There is due from the judge to the advocate some commendation and gracing,[15] where causes are well handled and fair pleaded, especially towards the side which obtaineth[16] not, for that upholds in the client the reputation of his counsel, and beats down in him the conceit[17] of his cause. There is likewise due to the public a civil reprehension of advocates, where there appeareth cunning counsel, gross neglect, slight information, indiscreet pressing, or an over-bold defense. And let not the counsel at the bar chop[18] with the judge, nor wind himself into the handling of the cause anew after the judge hath declared his sentence; but, on the other side, let not the judge meet the cause half way, nor give occasion for the party to say his counsel or proofs were not heard. 80

Thirdly, for that that concerns clerks and ministers. The place of justice is an hallowed place, and therefore not only the bench, but the foot-pace[19] and precincts and purprise[20] thereof ought to be preserved without scandal and corruption. For certainly, "Grapes," as the Scripture saith, "will not be gathered of thorns or thistles"; neither can justice yield her fruit with sweetness amongst the briars and brambles of catching[21] and polling[22] clerks and ministers. The attendance of courts is subject to four bad instruments. First, certain persons that are sowers of suits, which make the court swell, and the country pine. The second sort is of those that engage courts in quarrels of jurisdiction, and are not truly *amici curiæ,* but *parasiti curiæ* [not friends but parasites of the court], in puffing a court up beyond her bounds, for their own scraps and advantage. The third sort is of those that may be accounted the left hands of courts: persons that are full of nimble and sinister tricks and shifts, whereby they pervert the plain and direct courses of courts, and bring justice into oblique lines and labyrinths. And the fourth is the poller[23] and exacter of fees; which justifies the common resemblance of the courts of justice to the bush whereunto while the sheep flies for defense in 90 100

15. Favor. 16. Wins. 17. Opinion. 18. Bandy words, altercate. 19. Carpet or dais. 20. Barrier or enclosure. 21. Rapacious. 22. Plundering. 23. Plunderer.

110 weather,[24] he is sure to lose part of his fleece. On the other side, an ancient clerk, skillful in precedents, wary in proceeding, and understanding in the business of the court, is an excellent finger of a court, and doth many times point the way to the judge himself.

Fourthly, for that which may concern the sovereign and estate. Judges ought above all to remember the conclusion of the Roman Twelve Tables,[25] *Salus populi suprema lex* [The welfare of the people is the supreme law]; and to know that laws, except they be in order to that end, are but things cap-
120 tious, and oracles not well inspired. Therefore it is an happy thing in a state when kings and states do often consult with judges, and again when judges do often consult with the king and state: the one, when there is matter of law intervenient in business of state; the other, when there is some consideration of state intervenient in matter of law. For many times the things deduced to judgment may be *meum* and *tuum* [mine and thine], when the reason and consequence thereof may trench to point of estate: [26] I call matter of estate, not only the parts of sovereignty but whatsoever introduceth any great al-
130 teration or dangerous precedent or concerneth manifestly any great portion of people. And let no man weakly conceive that just laws and true policy have any antipathy, for they are like the spirits and sinews, that one moves with the other. Let judges also remember that Solomon's throne was supported by lions on both sides: let them be lions, but yet lions under the throne, being circumspect that they do not check or oppose any points of sovereignty. Let not judges also be so ignorant of their own right, as to think there is not left to them, as a principal part of their office, a wise use and application of
140 laws. For they may remember what the apostle [27] saith of a greater law than theirs: *Nos scimus quia lex bona est, modo quis ea utatur legitime* [We know that law is good, if a man use it lawfully].

24. Rough weather. 25. Laws put forth in 451-450 B.C. and used as a basis of Roman jurisprudence. However, the quotation is not from them but from Cicero. 26. The matters brought for judgment may be questions of property, but the principle and consequences involved may extend into particular matters concerning the state. 27. St. Paul.

LVII. OF ANGER

To seek to extinguish anger utterly is but a bravery [1] of the Stoics.[2] We have better oracles: "Be angry, but sin not." "Let not the sun go down upon your anger." Anger must be limited and confined both in race [3] and in time. We will first speak how the natural inclination and habit to be angry may be attempered and calmed; secondly, how the particular motions of anger may be repressed or at least refrained from doing mischief; thirdly, how to raise anger or appease anger in another.

For the first: there is not other way but to meditate and ruminate well upon the effects of anger, how it troubles man's life. And the best time to do this is to look back upon anger when the fit is thoroughly over. Seneca saith well, "That anger is like ruin, which breaks itself upon that it falls." The Scripture exhorteth us "to possess our souls in patience." Whosoever is out of patience is out of possession of his soul. Men must not turn bees,

. . . animasque in vulnere ponunt

[and put their lives in the sting].

Anger is certainly a kind of baseness; as it appears well in the weakness of those subjects in whom it reigns: children, women, old folks, sick folks. Only men must beware that they carry their anger rather with scorn than with fear, so that they may seem rather to be above the injury than below it; which is a thing easily done if a man will give law to himself in it.

For the second point: the causes and motives of anger are chiefly three. First, to be too sensible of hurt, for no man is angry that feels not himself hurt; and therefore tender and delicate persons must needs be oft angry: they have so many things to trouble them which more robust natures have little sense of. The next is the apprehension and construction [4] of the injury offered to be, in the circumstances thereof, full of contempt, for contempt is that which putteth an edge upon

1. Pretension, vaunt. 2. See II, n. 14. 3. Course. 4. Interpretation.

anger as much or more than the hurt itself. And therefore when men are ingenious in picking out circumstances of contempt, they do kindle their anger much. Lastly, opinion of the touch of a man's reputation [5] doth multiply and sharpen anger. Wherein the remedy is, that a man should have, as Consalvo [6] was wont to say, *telam honoris crassiorem* [a good strong web of honor]. But in all refrainings [7] of anger, it is the best remedy to win time and to make a man's self believe that the opportunity of his revenge is not yet come, but that he foresees a time for it; and so to still himself in the meantime, and reserve it.

To contain [8] anger from mischief, though it take hold of a man, there be two things whereof you must have special caution. The one, of extreme bitterness of words, especially if they be aculeate [9] and proper; [10] for *communia maledicta* [general aspersions] are nothing so much; and again, that in anger a man reveal no secrets, for that makes him not fit for society. The other, that you do not peremptorily break off in any business in a fit of anger; but howsoever you show bitterness, do not act anything that is not revocable.

For raising and appeasing anger in another: it is done chiefly by choosing of times, when men are frowardest and worst disposed, to incense them. Again, by gathering (as was touched before) all that you can find out to aggravate the contempt. And the two remedies are by the contraries. The former to take good times, when first to relate to a man an angry business, for the first impression is much; and the other is to sever, as much as may be, the construction of the injury from the point of contempt, imputing it to misunderstanding, fear, passion, or what you will.

5. That a man's reputation has been affected. 6. Hernandez de Cordova, Spanish general, d. 1515. 7. Restraints. 8. Hold back. 9. Stinging. 10. Personal.

LVIII. OF VICISSITUDE OF THINGS

Solomon saith, "There is no new thing upon the earth." So that as Plato had an imagination, "That all knowledge was but remembrance," so Solomon giveth his sentence,[1] "That all novelty is but oblivion." Whereby you may see that the river of Lethe [2] runneth as well above ground as below. There is an abstruse astrologer that saith, "If it were not for two things that are constant (the one is that the fixed stars ever stand at like distance one from another and never come nearer together nor go further asunder; the other, that the diurnal motion perpetually keepeth time), no individual would last one moment." Certain it is that the matter is in a perpetual flux,[3] and never at a stay. The great winding-sheets, that bury all things in oblivion, are two: deluges and earthquakes. As for conflagrations and great droughts, they do not merely [4] dispeople and destroy. Phaëton's [5] car went but a day. And the three years' drought in the time of Elias [6] was but particular,[7] and left people alive. As for the great burnings by lightnings, which are often in the West Indies,[8] they are but narrow.[9] But in the other two destructions, by deluge and earthquake, it is further to be noted, that the remnant of people which hap [10] to be reserved, are commonly ignorant and mountainous people, that can give no account of the time past, so that the oblivion is all one as if none had been left. If you consider well of the people of the West Indies, it is very probable that they are a newer or a younger people than the people of the Old World. And it is much more likely that the destruction that hath heretofore been there was not by earthquakes (as the Egyptian priest told Solon [11] concerning the island of

1. Opinion. 2. River in Hades whose waters, when drunk, caused complete forgetfulness. 3. Succession of changes. 4. Utterly. 5. Sun of Helios, god of the sun in Greek mythology (called Sol by the Romans but sometimes confused with Apollo). Phaethon set heaven and earth on fire in an attempt to drive his father's chariot. Zeus, king of the gods, killed him with a thunderbolt. 6. Elijah, prophet of Jehovah about 900 B.C. See I *Kings,* xvii and xviii. 7. Partial. 8. America in general. 9. Limited. 10. Happen. 11. Athenian lawgiver and Sage, d. 558 B.C.

Atlantis,[12] "that it was swallowed by an earthquake"), but
30 rather that it was desolated by a particular [13] deluge. For earthquakes are seldom in those parts. But on the other side, they have such pouring rivers as [14] the rivers of Asia and Africk and Europe are but brooks to them. Their Andes, likewise, or mountains, are far higher than those with us; whereby it seems that the remnants of generation of men were in such a particular deluge saved. As for the observation that Machiavel [15] hath,[16] that the jealousy of sects doth much extinguish the memory of things, traducing Gregory the Great,[17] that he did what in him lay to extinguish all heathen antiquities, I do
40 not find that those zeals do any great effects, nor last long; as it appeared in the succession of Sabiniah,[18] who did revive the former antiquities.

The vicissitude or mutations in the superior globe [19] are no fit matter for this present argument. It may be, Plato's great year,[20] if the world should last so long, would have some effect, not in renewing the state of like [21] individuals (for that is the fume [22] of those that conceive the celestial bodies have more accurate influences upon these things below than indeed they have), but in gross. Comets, out of question,[23] have like-
50 wise power and effect over the gross and mass of things, but they are rather gazed upon and waited upon in their journey, than wisely observed in their effects, specially in their respective [24] effects; that is, what kind of comet, for magnitude, color, version [25] of the beams, placing in the region of heaven, or lasting, produceth what kind of effects.

There is a toy [26] which I have heard, and I would not have it given over, but waited upon [27] a little. They say it is observed in the Low Countries (I know not in what part) that

12. Mythical continent said to have been engulfed by that Atlantic ocean. 13. Confined to a limited space. 14. That. 15. Florentine statesman and writer on politics, d. 1527. 16. Makes. 17. Pope Gregory the Great, d. 604. Machiavelli states that Gregory ordered the destruction of poems, histories, and idols connected with pagan superstitions. (*Discourses,* II, 5.) 18. Succeeded Gregory as Pope; under him there was some revival of paganism. 19. Upper sphere, heavens. See I, n. 14. 20. The time required for all heavenly bodies to revolve to the places they had at the beginning of the world. 21. Identical or similar. 22. Notion. 23. Without doubt. 24. Different. 25. Turning round. 26. Trifle. 27. Noted.

every five and thirty years the same kind and suit[28] of years and weathers comes about again, as great frosts, great wet, 60 great droughts, warm winters, summers with little heat, and the like; and they call it the *Prime*. It is a thing I do the rather mention, because, computing backwards, I have found some concurrence.

But to leave these points of nature, and to come to men. The greatest vicissitude of things amongst men is the vicissitude of sects and religions. For those orbs[29] rule in men's minds most. The true religion is "built upon the rock"; the rest are tossed upon the waves of time. To speak,[30] therefore, of the causes of new sects, and to give some counsel concern- 70 ing them, as far as the weakness of human judgment can give stay to so great revolutions.

When the religion formerly received is rent by discords, and when the holiness of the professors of religion is decayed and full of scandal, and withal the times be stupid, ignorant, and barbarous, you may doubt[31] the springing up of a new sect, if then also there should arise any extravagant and strange spirit to make himself author thereof. All which points held when Mahomet published his law. If a new sect have not two properties, fear it not, for it will not spread. The one is the 80 supplanting or the opposing of authority established, for nothing is more popular than that. The other is the giving license to pleasures and a voluptuous life. For as for speculative heresies (such as were in ancient times the Arians,[32] and now the Arminians[33]), though they work mightily upon men's wits,[34] yet they do not produce any great alterations in states, except it be by the help of civil[35] occasions. There be three manner of plantations of new sects:[36] by the power of signs and miracles, by the eloquence and wisdom of speech and persuasion, and by the sword. For martyrdoms, I reckon them 90

28. Sequence. 29. Spheres (e.g. *Primum Mobile*); apparently used metaphorically for *motives*. 30. It remains for me to speak. 31. Fear. 32. Sect founded in the 4th century by Arius, who denied that God the Father and God the Son are equal in the Christian Trinity. 33. Followers of Arminius (Jakob Harmensen, d. 1609), a Dutch Protestant theologian who objected to the doctrine that God predestined the salvation or damnation of individuals before their creation. Arminius taught that a man was damned if he freely rejected the mercy of Christ. 34. Minds. 35. Political. 36. Three ways in which new sects may be set up.

amongst miracles, because they seem to exceed the strength of human nature, and I may do the like of superlative and admirable holiness of life. Surely there is no better way to stop the rising of new sects and schisms than to reform abuses, to compound the smaller differences, to proceed mildly and not with sanguinary persecutions, and rather to take off the principal authors by winning and advancing them than to enrage them by violence and bitterness.

The changes and vicissitude in wars are many, but chiefly 100 in three things: in the seats or stages of the war, in the weapons, and in the manner of the conduct. Wars in ancient time seemed more to move from east to west, for the Persians, Assyrians, Arabians, Tartars (which were the invaders) were all eastern people. It is true, the Gauls were western, but we read but of two incursions of theirs: the one to Gallo-Grecia,[37] the other to Rome. But east and west have no certain points of heaven,[38] and no more have the wars, either from the east or west, any certainty of observation. But north and south are fixed; and it hath seldom or never been seen that the far south- 110 ern people have invaded the northern, but contrariwise. Whereby it is manifest that the northern tract of the world is in nature the more martial region, be it in respect [39] of the stars of that hemisphere, or of the great continents that are upon the north; whereas the south part, for aught that is known, is almost all sea; or [40] (which is most apparent) of the cold of the northern parts, which is that which, without aid of discipline, doth make the bodies hardest, and the courages warmest.

Upon the breaking and shivering of a great state and em- 120 pire, you may be sure to have wars. For great empires, while they stand, do enervate and destroy the forces of the natives which they have subdued, resting upon their own protecting forces; and then when they fail also, all goes to ruin, and they become a prey. So was it in the decay of the Roman empire; and likewise in the empire of Almaigne,[41] after Charles the Great,[42] every bird taking a feather; and were not unlike to

37. Galatia, in Asia Minor. 38. I.e., east and west are not pointed out in the heavens by a particular star or stars in the way that north is fixed and pointed out by the polar star. 39. Whether it is because. 40. Or whether it is because. 41. Germany. 42. Charlemagne, d. 814, king of the Franks and Roman emperor.

befall to Spain, if it should break. The great accessions and unions of kingdoms do likewise stir up wars, for when a state grows to an over-power, it is like a great flood that will be sure to overflow, as it hath been seen in the states of Rome, Turkey, 130 Spain, and others. Look when the world hath fewest barbarous peoples, but such as commonly will not marry or generate, except they know means to live (as it is almost everywhere at this day, except Tartary), there is no danger of inundations of people: but when there be great shoals of people, which go on to populate, without foreseeing means of life and sustentation, it is of necessity that once in an age or two they discharge a portion of their people upon other nations; which the ancient northern people were wont to do by lot, casting lots what part should stay at home, and what should seek their fortunes. 140 When a warlike state grows soft and effeminate, they may be sure of a war, for commonly such states are grown rich in the time of their degenerating; and so the prey inviteth, and their decay in valor encourageth a war.

As for the weapons, it hardly falleth under rule and observation; yet we see even they have returns and vicissitudes. For certain it is, that ordnance [43] was known in the city of the Oxidrakes in India, and was that which the Macedonians called thunder and lightning, and magic. And it is well known that the use of ordnance hath been in China above two thousand 150 years. The conditions of weapons, and their improvement, are: First, the fetching afar off,[44] for that outruns the danger, as it is seen in ordnance and muskets. Secondly, the strength of the percussion, wherein likewise ordnance do exceed all arietations [45] and ancient inventions. The third is the commodious use of them, as that they may serve in all weathers, that the carriage may be light and manageable, and the like.

For the conduct of the war: at the first, men rested [46] extremely upon number: they did put the wars likewise upon main force and valor, pointing [47] days for pitched fields [48] and 160 so trying it out upon an even match; and they were more ignorant in ranging and arraying their battles. After they grew to rest upon number rather competent than vast, they grew to

43. Gunpowder. 44. Hitting from a distance. 45. Attacks with battering-rams. 46. Depended. 47. Appointing. 48. Pitched battles (i.e. sides ranged in formal battle-order with equal forces).

advantages of place, cunning diversions, and the like; and they grew more skillful in the ordering of their battles.

In the youth of a state, arms do flourish; in the middle age of a state, learning; and then both of them together for a time; in the declining age of a state, mechanical arts and merchandize. Learning hath his [49] infancy, when it is but beginning 170 and almost childish; then his youth, when it is luxuriant and juvenile; then his strength of years, when it is solid and reduced; [50] and lastly, his old age, when it waxeth dry and exhaust.[51] But it is not good to look too long upon these turning wheels of vicissitude, lest we become giddy. As for the philology [52] of them, that is but a circle of tales, and therefore not fit for this writing.

A FRAGMENT OF AN ESSAY ON FAME

The poets make Fame [1] a monster; they describe her in part finely and elegantly, and in part gravely and sententiously; [2] they say, "Look how many feathers she hath; so many eyes she hath underneath; so many tongues; so many voices; she pricks up so many ears."

This is a flourish: [3] there follow excellent parables: [4] as that she gathereth strength in going; that she goeth upon the ground, and yet hideth her head in the clouds; that in the day-time she sitteth in a watch-tower, and flieth most by night; 10 that she mingleth things done with things not done; and that she is a terror to great cities. But that which passeth all the rest is, they do recount that the Earth, mother of the giants that made war against Jupiter, and were by him destroyed, thereupon in anger brought forth Fame. For certain it is that rebels, figured [5] by the giants, and seditious fames and libels, are but brothers and sisters, masculine and feminine. But now if a man can tame this monster, and bring her to feed at the hand, and govern her, and with her fly [6] other ravening [7] fowl and kill them, it is somewhat worth. But we are infected with

49. Its. 50. Disciplined, condensed. 51. Exhausted. 52. B. apparently means *the history*. 1. Rumor. 2. With rich meaning. 3. An embellishment. 4. Comparisons. 5. Typified. 6. Attack. 7. Predatory.

the style of the poets. To speak now in a sad[8] and serious manner, there is not in all the politics[9] a place less handled and more worthy to be handled than this of fame. We will therefore speak of these points: what are false fames, and what are true fames, and how they may be best discerned;[10] how fames may be sown and raised, how they may be spread and multiplied, and how they may be checked and laid dead; and other things concerning the nature of fame. 20

Fame is of that force, as[11] there is scarcely any great action wherein it hath not a great part, especially in the war. Mucianus undid[12] Vitellius by a fame that he scattered, that Vitellius had in purpose to move the legions of Syria into Germany, and the legions of Germany into Syria; whereupon the legions of Syria were infinitely inflamed. Julius Cæsar took Pompey unprovided, and laid asleep his industry and preparations by a fame that he cunningly gave out, how Cæsar's own soldiers loved him not, and being wearied with the wars, and laden with the spoils of Gaul, would forsake him as soon as he came into Italy. Livia[13] settled all things for the succession of her son Tiberius, by continually giving out that her husband Augustus was upon recovery and amendment; and it is a usual thing with the bashaws[14] to conceal the death of the Great Turk from the janizaries[15] and men of war, to save the sacking of Constantinople and other towns, as their manner is. Themistocles made Xerxes, King of Persia, post apace out of Grecia,[16] by giving out that the Grecians had a purpose to break his bridge of ships which he had made athwart the Hellespont. There be a thousand such like examples; and the more they are, the less they need to be repeated, because a man meeteth with them everywhere. Therefore, let all wise governors have as great a watch and care over fames as they have of the actions and designs themselves. 30 40 50

8. Grave. 9. The science of politics. 10. Distinguished. 11. That. 12. Ruined. 13. See V, n. 4. 14. Turkish officials. 15. Bodyguard for Turkish sultans. 16. Greece.

Bibliography

Bacon's works are readily available in various editions and texts. The following are recommended:

Works, 7 vols., ed. Spedding, Ellis and Heath. (Contains the complete works of Bacon, both in Latin and English; translations are also provided.)

The Philosophical Works, ed. J. M. Robertson. (Reprinted from the above.)

Essays, Advancement of Learning, New Atlantis, and Other Pieces, ed. R. F. Jones. (A useful collection of Bacon's most interesting writings.)

Biographies of Bacon are numerous. Those by Church, Abbott, and Lovejoy are probably too harsh in their treatment of his character. The following are recommended:

James Spedding, *The Letters and Life of Francis Bacon,* 7 vols.

John Nichol, *Francis Bacon, His Life and Philosophy.*

Mary Sturt, *Francis Bacon, A Biography.*

Charles Williams, *Bacon.*

Sir Sidney Lee, "Bacon" in *Great Englishmen of the Sixteenth Century.*

The following criticisms will be of use to students: the articles by Gardiner and Fowler in the *Dictionary of National Biography;* by Macmillan in *International Journal of Ethics* for October, 1906; by Crane in *Schelling Anniversary Papers;* by Zeitlin in *JEGP* for 1928; by McMahon in *PMLA* for 1945; and by Allbutt in *Proceedings of the British Academy* for 1913. For the essay genre, the following are recommended: E. N. S. Thompson, *The Seventeenth Century Essay;* and *Century Readings in the English Essay,* ed. Louis Wann.